REX STOUT

REX STOUT

David R. Anderson

Frederick Ungar Publishing Co.
New York

For my mother and father
earliest and best of teachers

Copyright © 1984 by Frederick Ungar Publishing Co., Inc.

Printed in the United States of America

Library of Congress Cataloging in Publication Data

Anderson, David R., 1952–
  Rex Stout.

  (Recognitions)
  Bibliography: p.
  Includes index.
  1. Stout, Rex, 1886–1975—Criticism and interpretation.
  2. Stout, Rex, 1886–1975—Characters—Nero Wolfe.
  3. Detective and mystery stories, American—History and
  criticism. I. Title. II. Series.
  PS3537.T733Z52 1984   813'.52   84-130
  ISBN 0-8044-2005-X
  ISBN 0-8044-6009-4 (pbk.)

Contents

Preface

This is a study of Rex Stout's Nero Wolfe novels. It excludes most of his other writing, including the Nero Wolfe novellas and short stories, Stout's crime fiction which features other detectives, his "serious" novels, and the vast body of his political writing—pamphlets, speeches, and so forth, as well as his journalism and other occasional pieces. Since not all the Nero Wolfe novels could be analyzed in a book of this length, I have focused on the ones I regard as the most important and the best. Those readers who are new to the world of Nero Wolfe and Archie Goodwin will find the other novels listed in the selected bibliography at the end of this book. The seasoned Stout reader will, I hope, think of many examples from the other Wolfe novels to support my arguments here but none to contradict it.

In writing about Rex Stout I have benefited from the kindness and generosity of both individuals and institutions. My greatest debt is to John J. McAleer, Rex Stout's biographer, who first introduced me to the Nero Wolfe novels ten years ago and first encouraged me to write about them. In the intervening years he has helped me with this and other projects in many ways, and I am deeply grateful. I must also thank Bruce Cassiday for his helpful reading of the manuscript, Mark Anderson for the loan of his Rex Stout Collection, and Keith Bryant, Dean of the College of Liberal Arts, and David Stewart, Head of the Department of English at Texas A&M University, for a course reduction which freed me to write.

The Office of University Research at Texas A&M, the Special Collections department of the Boston College Libraries, and the

Humanities Research Center at the University of Texas—Austin also aided me in my research.

Above all, thanks to my wife Priscilla for being so literate and so loving.

D. R. A.

Bryan, Texas
June, 1983

Chronology

1886   RS born on December 1 in Noblesville, Indiana.

1887   Stout family moves to Kansas where RS grew up, first in Wakarusa, then in Bellview, finally in Topeka.

1905   RS joins navy. Assigned as pay-yeoman aboard Presidential yacht *Mayflower*.

1907   RS discharged from navy. Roams country working at various jobs. Finally settles in New York in 1908.

1911   RS spends year wandering the country, working at odd jobs.

1912   Returns to New York. Devotes himself full-time to writing for popular magazines.

1916   Marries Fay Kennedy. Helps found Educational Thrift Service.

1926   Leaves ETS with financial security. Determined to write serious fiction.

1927   RS abroad, traveling and writing.

1929   Publishes *How Like a God*, first novel published in book form. Returns to US and builds High Meadow, his home for the rest of his life.

1932   Marries Pola Weinbach Hoffman, having divorced first wife in 1931.

1934   Publishes *Fer-de-Lance*, first Nero Wolfe novel, in October. In next five prolific years writes more Wolfe novels, other crime fiction, other kinds of fiction.

1941   Helps found Fight for Freedom Committee and Freedom House as war issues take up more and more of his time.

1942   Heads Writer's War Board. Almost completely gives up fiction for duration of war. Returns to New York city from High Meadow to head up propaganda effort.

1

"To Write Profound Things . . . ": Rex Stout's Life

Rex Stout, the creator of Nero Wolfe, was in the course of his long and varied life a shrewd businessman, a relentless propagandist, a tireless political activist, and an old-fashioned individualist. He was the sort of man one calls a "character"—brilliant, fierce, self-sustained, and yet warm and humane. Above all, though, he was a writer, and the world he imagined and brought into being has won its place in our literature for its witty, engaging, and ultimately moving treatment of crime fiction's great theme: the struggle between order and disorder.

Rex Todhunter Stout was born December 1, 1886 in Noblesville, Indiana to John Wallace and Lucetta Todhunter Stout.[1] His father was co-owner of the local newspaper, the *Noblesville Republican-Ledger*, but after two successive undependable partners he was forced to sell out. Thus, it happened that when Rex was only eight months old the Stout family moved to Kansas, where they eventually settled on a forty-acre farm outside the town of Wakarusa, just south of Topeka. It was here that Rex Stout spent his boyhood.

Of the Stouts' nine children, four boys and five girls, Rex was the sixth. During the Wakarusa years, he and his brothers and sisters shared most of the farm chores, attended school together, and—perhaps their favorite activity—staged elaborate home dramatic performances featuring original scripts. Alone, Rex played in the fields, day-dreamed in the family's twenty-acre woodlot, and read hungrily. It was an active, happy childhood. Late in life Stout recalled, "Wakarusa! I doubt if anyone has ever had a more satisfactory early boyhood than mine there."[2]

1

A farm may be the best place to grow up—certainly Rex Stout felt it was—but life in the Stout family could not have been perfectly serene. After the move to Kansas, John Stout rapidly became superintendent of schools for all of Shawnee county, a job which kept him away from home except on weekends. His children remember him as fair-minded but also hot-tempered and over-disciplined. When attending the theater, for example, he insisted on arriving when the doors opened rather than at curtain time.[3] Because he was gone so often, because of his temper, and because of his rigidity, the Stout children feared their father at the same time they loved him. Rex's mother, a brilliant, eccentric woman, was cold-hearted. She loved to read, and to make time for her books she would sit in the kitchen, reading, with a bowl of cold water at her elbow. Any child who came up to speak to her had to submit to a face-washing first.[4] Hesitant to show too much affection, she lived by the rule, "Never praise or blame anyone."[5] With their absent father and indifferent mother, the Stout children were forced into a premature self-reliance. Furthermore, John and Lucetta grew apart. During the last twenty-five years of their marriage, in fact, though they lived together, they never spoke to each other, communicating only through their children. This deep-freeze had not set in at Wakarusa, but the tensions that presaged it must have been felt by all.

As much as possible for a young boy on a Kansas farm at the turn of the century, Rex Stout led the life of the mind. His father owned 1,126 books, and by the age of eleven Rex had read them all—including the Bible by the age of four. At eleven he was spelling champion of Kansas, Nebraska, and Illinois. At twelve he had read all of Shakespeare and knew the sonnets by heart. In 1896, after the family moved to Bellview, a larger town nearer Topeka, Rex was taken on a tour of Kansas schools to exhibit his amazing ability to add long columns of numbers rapidly in his head. The family moved again—this time to Topeka—in 1899, and Rex entered high school there at the age of thirteen. He knew Chaucer, Erasmus, Montaigne, Bunyan, Swift, and Pope. His favorite novels were *Anna Karenina* and *The Human Comedy*.[6]

Growing up with the Stouts meant not only soaking up knowledge in John Stout's library but also developing one's wits in discussion. John Stout never punished a child until the offender had had a chance to explain himself. These sessions at the bar honed Rex Stout's reasoning powers and verbal ability. The family theatricals, written and produced at home, called for creative energy and common sense. The environment was enriching in other ways, too. John Stout was involved in politics. Lucetta worked for the Temperance Union. David Overmeyer, John Stout's cousin, was a state legislator and candidate for Congress during Rex's boyhood. He brought William Jennings Bryan to Topeka, and Rex sat on his knee.

Thus, when he graduated from Topeka High in 1903, Rex Stout had a mind both developed and informed along with a country boyhood—just the right combination of sophistication and practicality. A few weeks at the University of Kansas in Lawrence convinced him that he already knew more than most of the students there, so he took a bookkeeping job, ushered in the evenings at Crawford's Opera House in Topeka so he could see first-run plays, and waited for something to happen.

Nothing did, so in 1905 Rex Stout joined the navy. A landlocked midwesterner in search of adventure on a paltry budget, he could think of no other way to see the world so cheaply. After a brief training period at Brooklyn Naval Yard and then at Norfolk, Stout found himself assigned to Theodore Roosevelt's presidential yacht, the *Mayflower*. As pay-yeoman, among other duties he audited Roosevelt's entertainment bills to see which expenses Roosevelt should pay and which he could pass on to the government. But Stout saw more than ledgers. The *Mayflower* sailed to Puerto Rico, Guantanamo, Havana, the Canal Zone, French Guiana, Barbados, Port-au-Prince, Martinique, and Argentina, in addition to sailing up and down the eastern seaboard of America. Finally, however, ship life became too confining, and after two years Yeoman Stout bought his discharge in 1907, expressing a desire to study law.

Stout studied law for two months in Cleveland, after which he clerked in a cigar store, kept books for the Cleveland Street Railway Company, and took jobs briefly in Indianapolis, Norfolk, Virginia, and Springfield, Illinois. Finally, in the summer of 1908 he moved to New York and took another bookkeeping job. It was immediately after his enlistment in the navy that Rex Stout had first seen New York—the buildings, the books, the concert halls, the celebrities, the theaters. He must have known then that he was destined for the city, his sailing and itinerant bookkeeping merely a prelude to his settling there. But while Stout had been busy traveling, his family had been moving too—nearly all of them eastward. In 1909 Rex and his brother Bob wrote to Indianapolis where his sister Ruth, his brother Donald, and his mother lived, inviting them all to move to New York. They did. The next year, his father joined them, and once again his father and mother were together. It was at this point that Lucetta Stout ceased speaking to her husband, blaming him for the death of their daughter Mary, who died in 1908, in a deep depression, of what was diagnosed as heart failure. Rex, as if to make up for the silence at home, supported himself as a barker on a tour bus, promoting the sights of New York to out-of-towners like himself.

The year 1911 was a remarkable one for Rex Stout. Apparently, his voyages on the *Mayflower* had not satisfied his wanderlust, for in the twelve months of that year he lived in twelve different states. In Pittsburgh, New Orleans, Albuquerque, Colorado Springs, Spokane, Duluth, Chicago, Butte, Helena, Laramie, and St. Louis, he worked at various jobs, among them fishing on a shrimp boat, managing a hotel, and keeping books. This was his last year of freedom before a five-year stint of writing for the popular magazines, and he used it to explore, experience, and expand. He may not have been consciously preparing for a writing career, but his travels served him well. "I never had any adventures," Stout later observed of this itinerant year, "but I had a lot of episodes. It was not only good preparation for a writer, but also for life."[7]

In 1912 Stout was back at bookkeeping in New York, his goal to save enough money so that he could devote himself full-time to writing. Up until now he had written only sporadically. He had sold a poem to *The Smart Set* at the age of seventeen, but it was never published. The *New York World* had published a feature piece on the palm prints of William Howard Taft and Cleveland mayor Tom Loftus Johnson, and *The Smart Set* had eventually published three of his poems in 1910 and 1911, but it was not until Eugene Manlove Rhodes, who wrote westerns for the *Saturday Evening Post*, visited the Stouts that Rex determined to write for a living. If a man like Rhodes could do it, he reasoned, he could too.[8] In the next five years Stout published thirty-two short stories and four novels. Mainly, he wrote for *All-Story*, which specialized in action and romance. At first he was paid a penny a word, then two and a half cents. He spent the checks as soon as he received them, and when the money was gone wrote some more. Many great writers have served hack apprenticeships—Samuel Johnson being a celebrated example—yet Stout did not seem particularly proud of his, for he kept no copies of this early work. It remained for his biographer, John McAleer, to rescue it and publish the cream as *'Justice Begins at Home' and Other Stories.*[9]

Rex Stout wrote his first crime fiction during his years at the pulps—"Justice Begins at Home," published in the December 4, 1915 issue of *All-Story*. For the most part, however, his stories and novels probe the interplay of intellect and emotion in human affairs—particularly in love. As such, they foreshadow important issues in the Wolfe novels. They also display a knack for dialogue and swift pacing, two of the most appealing qualities of his later work. For the most part, though, they are what they seem—works written under the constraints of the moment and motivated by the pressure of the purse. Recognizing this, Stout quit writing temporarily, determined not to write again until he had enough money to allow him to write seriously and with care. To amass that sum took twelve years.

In December, 1916, Rex Stout, whose writing up until then had focused on love and its relationship to the other emotions and to the intellect, married. His bride was Fay Kennedy of Topeka, sister of one of his high-school friends. Stout had not been carrying a torch for her during his New York years; she had come east on a visit, met Rex at breakfast, and simply renewed an old acquaintance. But marriage was not Stout's only important new venture in 1916, for in that year his brother Bob conceived the idea of Educational Thrift Service. For one-third ownership of the company, Rex Stout agreed to devise a method of operation for it and to implement that method.

The Educational Thrift Service worked through schools and banks simultaneously to encourage school children to open savings accounts. An ETS representative would come to a town and persuade the school administrators to start a savings program. At the same time, he would ask a local bank to participate. Then he would address the students on the virtues of thrift, ending with an invitation to join ETS. On a stated day every week or month students would bring their money to school and the school authorities would transfer it to the bank. Teachers and administrators approved of ETS because it taught thrift and because it required the students to do math and to develop a sense of civics. Banks liked it because it was a cheap source of advertising and was not inconvenient: ETS supplied the passbooks and other paraphernalia. The system grew rapidly, outstripping its competition until, by 1924, it practically ran itself. Rex Stout was free to pursue other activities while growing rich.

These other activities included financing a private printing of Casanova's *Memoirs*, hunting and fishing in Montana's mountains, and working with the American Civil Liberties Union. Through his ACLU connections Stout learned of a fledgling magazine, *The New Masses*, in which he invested $4,000 while agreeing to sit on its executive board. He became president of Vanguard Press during this period as well, a post he held until 1928. At this time, Stout's acquaintances and associates included members of New York's liberal intelligentsia—Scott Nearing, Thorstein Veblen, John Dos Passos, Egmont Arens—and its literary galaxy—Dos Passos, Dorothy Parker, Max Eastman, Carl Van Vechten, Joseph Wood Krutch, Mark and Carl Van Doren. It was heady company for a boy from Wakarusa, Kansas.

On his fortieth birthday, Stout informed his brother Bob that he wanted to sell his share of the company, and the following year he went to Europe to write, not as he had for the pulps— to keep food on the table—but as a serious novelist. The result was *How Like a God*, finished in 1929. After the mild success of this first novel, the Stouts returned to America, moving into a farmhouse in Brewster, New York, while Stout planned to build his dream house on eighteen acres of land he owned nearby, a tract that straddled the New York—Connecticut border.

The next five years saw the publication of four other novels which together with *How Like a God* constitute Stout's "serious" fiction, his attempt to compete with Faulkner, Hemingway, Conrad, and Woolf. *Seed On The Wind* (1930), *Golden Remedy* (1931), *Forest Fire* (1933), and *The President Vanishes* (1934) received mixed reviews in England and America. Respected writers and critics took them seriously, and Stout found himself mentioned in the same breath with other major American writers of the thirties, but his novels did not, finally, receive enough acclaim—or sell enough copies—to establish him as a major writer. Psychological studies of human behavior—of a woman who has babies out of wedlock to spite her father, of a forest ranger who unknowingly falls in love with a young man, of a philanderer who finds women disgusting—the early Stout novels reveal a continuing interest in the nature and denaturing of love and show a deepening inquiry into the conflict between reason and emotion. They experiment with point of view, narrative time, and psychology in fiction. But they have been overshadowed by the Nero Wolfe novels; nowadays, they are little read.

Like his work for the pulps, these years of writing for the critics form part of Stout's apprenticeship for what was to be his greatest achievement. Yet his most important activity during the early thirties was not literary, for it was during this period that he finally stopped roving and established a home. After the navy he had crossed the country, gaining experience, seeing sights, working different jobs. As a partner in ETS he had traveled extensively, setting up ETS programs at schools around the country. After the mid-twenties, secure in ETS, he had undertaken another kind of quest, leading a raucous social life in New York's literary and political worlds. Even his trip to Europe in the late twenties when he was writing *How Like a God* had represented a kind of rootless quest for tradition and history.

But during the thirties he moved to Brewster and began building High Meadow, his home for the rest of his life. Stout knew nothing of construction, yet with an equally uninformed crew of local men he built and furnished a fourteen-room house contoured to the side of a hill that looked over undeveloped countryside. With its eighteen acres, the house afforded an opportunity for the farm boy in him to reemerge. Soon Stout was growing vegetables, tending orchards, taming wild crows. High Meadow contained a study where he could write undisturbed and a swimming pool where he could relax. Instead of a noisy Manhattan apartment, he now lived in a world isolated, self-contained, and ordered. It afforded the perfect controlled environment for the creator of the Nero Wolfe stories. Part of the stability and order provided by High Meadow was due to a new inhabitant there. Stout and his wife Fay had agreed to a divorce in 1931. She preferred life in Manhattan to life at High Meadow, either not needing or taking no satisfaction in the stability Stout had created there. In 1932 he married Pola Weinbach, also recently divorced. Pola Stout, who became a distinguished designer of wool fabrics, loved High Meadow, family life, and Rex Stout. The stage was set for Nero Wolfe.

Rex Stout began writing *Fer-de-Lance*, the first Nero Wolfe novel, on October 18, 1933, the day after Pola returned home from the hospital with their first child, Barbara. Before Christmas, the novel was finished. Apart from the fact that his new home and family created a peaceful stability that allowed him to write, more practical considerations—some urgent, others more general—compelled Stout to write detective stories. For one thing, he needed the money. ETS, like the rest of the country, had suffered during the Depression, and without his organizational skill it had declined further, until his share of the profits no longer provided enough money to support a family of three in a new home. Furthermore, Stout was rethinking the direction of his literary career. For Stout, "To write profound things about the human soul your feelings about it have to be very deep, very difficult, as Dostoevsky's were, or Melville's, or Balzac's."[10] Stout knew that his were not. He was a very good writer, but he lacked the complex emotions necessary to be a great one. Recognizing this, he needed to decide what to write and what to expect from himself and his work, especially in light of his need to support himself and his family. He resolved to write detective novels. They sell well, they require good story telling, and they allow for the kind of authorial comment on character and society to which he was constitutionally inclined. He could excel in a genre suited to his talents and temper. This was not a sellout; it was finding the niche for which he had been searching—both as a person and as a writer—since his early days with the pulps.[11]

Before *Fer-de-Lance* appeared, Stout published *The President Vanishes*, a political thriller written after the Nero Wolfe novel and sold immediately to Hollywood. He published it anonymously, hoping that readers would ascribe it to a Washington insider. This technique worked, and the book sold well.[12] Shortly afterwards, in October, 1934, *The American Magazine* published an abridgement of *Fer-de-Lance*. Two days later, it appeared as a book. In the same month, Stout set to work on *The League of Frightened Men*, and a series was born. He was forty-eight years old.

The next five years were prolific ones. In addition to four Nero Wolfe novels—*The Rubber Band, The Red Box, Too Many Cooks*, and *Some Buried Caesar*—Stout published three other crime novels—*The Hand in the Glove, Red Threads*, and *Double for Death*—some light romantic novels—*O Careless Love* and *Mr. Cinderella*—and an adventure novel, *Mountain Cat*. Now, with no ETS income, Stout was supporting himself successfully and astonishing the public with his output.[13] It is difficult to say how long this might have kept up, or what effect it might have had on his writing, had it not been for Hitler's Germany.

In the years leading up to Pearl Harbor, and all during World War II, Stout was a vigorous propagandist, first for an early American entrance into the war and then, after Pearl Harbor, for the American war effort. His own writing did not halt abruptly in 1939; he published *Over My Dead Body* and *Where There's a Will* in 1940 and two Tecumseh Fox novels—*Bad for Business* and *The Broken Vase*—in 1940–41. Here, however, his output ceased until *The Silent Speaker* in 1946. Once he became involved in the war effort, Stout worked single-mindedly. He moved back to New York from High Meadow and set to work writing, taping radio programs, giving speeches, and chairing meetings, all in an attempt to bring the war rapidly to an end.

This flurry of political propagandizing began in April, 1941 with the formation of the Fight for Freedom Committee which Stout helped sponsor. He used the committee to attack neutralists, isolationists, and others opposed to America's entry into the war. This activity led, in October, 1941, to the founding of Freedom House, an organization dedicated to propagandizing for democracy with which Stout remained associated until his very last years.

One particular Freedom House project vexed the Nazi government so much it felt compelled to respond. Stout conducted

weekly fifteen-minute radio spots called "Our Secret Weapon"
in which he would dissect Nazi propaganda gathered by Freedom House researchers from sources in European print media
and radio. The program was broadcast in this country over CBS
beginning in August, 1942, and its aggressiveness and incisive-
ness so annoyed the Nazis that by November they responded.
Their propaganda machine reported that Rex Stout, "well-known
detective story writer and pulp magazine writer," had begun producing anti-Nazi propaganda. The announcer went on to betray
Nazi ignorance of the Wolfe series, however, with what was
meant to be an acid remark: "Now we have the explanation why
so many of the war stories released in Washington have so strong
a flavor of Chicago gangsterism."[14]

"Our Secret Weapon" and other Freedom House activities
kept Stout busy during these years, but the greatest demands on
his time and energy came from his leadership of the Writer's War
Board, founded as the Writer's War Committee in January, 1942.
This group of writers came together at the suggestion of the
Treasury Department to help sell war bonds, but by April, re-
named the Writer's War Board, it was producing radio dramas,
speeches, advertisements, poems, and a host of other things, all
in support of the war effort. Rex Stout did some writing himself,
and he was available for speeches and other appearances; mostly,
though, he ran the board much as he had run his part of ETS.
One of his tasks was to commission pieces from other writers,
and the War Board's list was impressive: Carl Sandburg, Mark
Van Doren, Joseph Wood Krutch, Pearl Buck, John Dos Passos,
Edna St. Vincent Millay, Clifford Odets, Robert Benchley, and
John P. Marquand, among others.[15]

Rex Stout was not a man who dealt in half measures; his life
testifies to his urge to perform every task, to hold every belief,
thoroughly or not at all. Perhaps it was this trait more than any
other that led him to the controversy over the guilt of the German
people which clouded his years on the Writer's War Board. Stout
personally goaded the Board to undertake a propaganda campaign designed to convince the American people that "the blame
for Hitler rested on the German people themselves."[16] To this
end, the Board commissioned a radio play on book burning in
Nazi Germany and similar works. Stout himself wrote a major

essay called "We Shall Hate or We Shall Fail" for the *New York Times Magazine* (January 17, 1943), standing firm against the flood of protests it elicited from theologians, civil libertarians, writers, and other readers. This intense anti-Germanic stance led, predictably, to the argument that at the end of the war Germany should be economically hobbled so that it could never threaten peace again. Among other things, Stout—a founding member of a new group called the Society for the Prevention of World War III—advocated the dismantling of Germany's chemical and metallurgical industries and their reestablishment in the countries Germany had invaded. This extension of his anti-Germanicism brought protests from old allies like John P. Marquand and Max Eastman as well as from such colleagues as Alfred Kazin, Frederick Lewis Allen, Muriel Rukeyser, and William L. White. It led also to tensions at the Writer's War Board and at Freedom House, where Stout and Dorothy Thompson so incensed each other with their attitudes on this issue that they both resigned. (Both later rejoined.)[17] Stout, a controversialist throughout the war, had succeeded in alienating more than the Nazis this time.

To some readers, an essay like "We Shall Hate or We Shall Fail," with its brutal title, seems the work of an unreasonable man, but another cause Stout took up at about this same time takes the edge off that brutality: he began a vigorous campaign for world government. This was to be his chief political cause during the postwar years. His point was that nations, in order to guarantee their safety, would have to give up a portion of their sovereignty to a world government, including, perhaps, an international peace force. Accordingly, in 1949 the Writer's War Board was reborn as the Writer's Board for World Peace, with Stout as its chairman. Its purpose, like that of the WWB, was to propagandize, this time not for war but for peace.

Stout took up another cause at the end of the war years— reprint royalties for authors. As a member both of the Author's League and the Author's Guild, he had been dismayed to see publishers of hardcover books investing more and more of their resources in the paperback reprint houses, which enabled them to republish an author's work at a lower price and to sell more copies without paying adequate royalties on the paperback sales.

Stout claimed that in a given year publishers would make $6,720,000 from cheap reprints; authors would get $600,000. After the war Stout also became as much a foe of communism as he had been of fascism. He even revived the format of his "Our Secret Weapon" broadcasts to expose Stalin's lies. At the time of the Zeck trilogy of the late forties, his absorption with the anti-communist crusade was clearly reflected in his novels. Nevertheless, Stout despised McCarthyism. His opposition to extremists on both political left and right shows that the activity which kept him so busy grew out of a hatred of totalitarianism in all its forms rather than out of demagoguery.

The year 1946 marked the resumption of the Nero Wolfe series. Early in the year Stout had returned to High Meadow and, even though he remained politically active in the causes that had grown up at the end of the war, devoted more time to his writing. During the war he had limited himself to one Wolfe novella a year. Now that he was back in harness, all the rest of his novels would be Nero Wolfe novels. For the next thirty years he would spend six or eight weeks a year writing one Nero Wolfe novel and one or two novellas; otherwise, he was his own man.

Nevertheless, in 1965 he was back in the public eye again over two controversial issues—the FBI and the war in Vietnam. *The Doorbell Rang*, published in 1965, attacked pretensions to infallibility by the FBI, in the person of J. Edgar Hoover. Stout deplored Hoover's tendency to shield himself and his agency from criticism—and even from inquiry—on the grounds that such activities were somehow unpatriotic. His most popular novel, *The Doorbell Rang*, struck a chord to which Americans of the sixties responded. His championing of the Vietnam war, however, was another matter. There cannot have been many Americans in the early sixties who thumbed their noses at the FBI in a novel, deplored the FBI's conduct of the Rosenberg investigation and trial in—of all places—*Ramparts* magazine, and yet supported the war, but Stout regarded these stands as consistent. He saw an unbridled FBI and a communist presence in Southeast Asia both as threats to personal freedom. Thus, he saw no contradiction in publishing, under the Freedom House banner in 1965, a statement which, while acknowledging the right to dissent, exhorted supporters of the war to come forth loudly. One of his cosigners was Richard Nixon.[18]

The next year, Freedom House gave its annual award to President Johnson, who used the occasion to defend his administration's Vietnam policy. Four thousand demonstrators picketed the awards dinner in New York. Inside the hotel where the banquet was taking place, Rex Stout, unaccustomed to retreating from a position he had taken and which had been challenged so publicly, reconfirmed his commitment to the war. It was an eerie replay of the controversy over his "We Shall Hate or We Shall Fail" stance. As the months and years went on, he found himself increasingly alone on this issue. As a compensation, his defense of the war effort became more and more heated, until Pola Stout had to call their close friends to ask that they avoid the topic. John McAleer suggests that a two-year bout with violent headaches which occurred at this time was due to Stout's tensions over the war issue.[19] In 1969 he wrote to President Nixon, the man he later called "unquestionably the greatest danger that ever occurred to American democracy," to express his support of Nixon's Vietnam policy.[20]

Rex Stout lived out his last years peacefully and quietly at High Meadow. His keen interest in politics continued unabated, piqued especially by the Watergate affair. He gave interviews. He read the *New York Times* thoroughly every day. Mostly, though, he absorbed himself in the world he had created. Rarely going out, except for family gatherings in the neighborhood, he worked in his garden, read, answered correspondence, and wrote. After suffering a broken back in a fall, he had a lift installed to take him up the stairs of his house. After a debilitating illness, he hired a secretary to help answer his mail and to type his manuscripts. He began to lose hearing in one ear and sight in one eye. But though his body decayed, he remained alert. *A Family Affair*, his last novel, was written just months before his death, yet in conception and performance it is one of his best.

When Rex Stout died on October 27, 1975, his body was cremated and the ashes scattered. His legacy was astonishing. At his death he had more books in print than any living American author. He counted among his readers the president of France, a member of the Vatican curia, and an Indian maharajah.[21] More

than that, he left a reputation as a warm, human, intelligent, free-
dom-loving man. He had loved and been loved. He had fought
Nazis and Communists. He had campaigned for justice. He had
fought for the economic rights of authors. Above all, he had written well. Who could ask for more?

2
The Struggle for Order: Overview of the Wolfe Saga

The Nero Wolfe novels offer more than just a collection of stories about the exploits of a detecting team, satisfying as such a collection would in itself be. Instead they form a unified whole, a cycle, a completed action. Stout produced a series detective, but his novels form more than a series—the whole is greater than the parts.

To begin with, continuity of character and setting provides unity in these novels. The brownstone on West Thirty-fifth Street is the setting for the opening scene of *Fer-de-Lance* and the closing scene of *A Family Affair,* and all of the intervening scenes owe something to the stability, solidity, and impregnability of the world represented by that structure. When Wolfe leaves it, as he does for example in *In the Best Families,* the story leans back towards the abandoned home. When Wolfe is there, the story draws strength from the order, the routine, the assumptions behind an establishment like Wolfe's. Its force is centripetal. Similarly, after some initial experimentation with minor characters like Johnny Keems and Bill Gore, Stout settled into a world in which the inhabitants of the brownstone and their associates remain as fixed and stable as the building itself. The more we see of them and the more we learn of them, the more credible and familiar their world becomes. A writer can create a world in one novel—as Stout did in *Fer-de-Lance*—but to return to that world and develop it over forty-one years makes it more than just a fictive world; it becomes a fictive home.

The Wolfe novels follow a cycle of engagement and disengagement with the world outside the brownstone. The killer in

Stout's first novel, *Fer-de-Lance*, tries to murder Wolfe in his own home, his refuge. This act of aggression requires Wolfe to acknowledge and to struggle with the forces outside his ordered home. His secluded order attacked, Wolfe must act to save it, and thus a pattern is begun. Over the next fifteen years, Wolfe continues to act, his engagement with the world climaxing in his battle with Arnold Zeck, his Moriarty, from 1949–51. The Zeck trilogy climaxes his engagement because it draws him out of the brownstone entirely; it constitutes the apogee of the orbit of the Wolfe novels, for here Wolfe is farthest from his center as he lurks in California, waiting to strike back. The end of the Wolfe saga is marked by the completion of the cycle. Once again, violence invades the brownstone, but this time it is an intimate violence, one that Wolfe cannot leave home to face. The action eventually leaves Wolfe radically disengaged—suspended from his profession, mute to the police, mute to Archie Goodwin. When the killer finally murders himself on the front steps of the brownstone, Wolfe—the crusader of the Zeck novels—is once again the hermit of Thirty-fifth Street.

Within this larger pattern of excursion and return embracing the entire Wolfe cycle, a smaller pattern repeats itself, giving coherence to each novel and meaning to the cycle. This is the pattern of order violated, order restored, the archetype for crime fiction. By repeating this pattern in each novel, Stout creates a prolonged struggle between social and moral order—which in crime fiction tend to be fundamentally the same—and the forces that threaten them. This struggle constitutes the basic conflict dramatized by the Wolfe cycle, while the larger pattern of excursion and return serves to link Wolfe's private world with the social world as this struggle continues. Wolfe cannot order his own world and then ignore what lies outside his door, for that world always forces its way in. Thus, Wolfe moves out to combat the world on its ground before returning to that struggle in his own world. His mute isolation from the world in *A Family Affair* will not work and cannot last. The cycle must begin again.

Rex Stout was not a theorist. A man of action in all spheres of life, he apparently found little satisfaction in abstractions. Certainly this holds true for his theory of crime fiction. His discussions of the subject are few, brief, and usually directed to a specific audience or occasion. Nevertheless a clear sense of Stout's theory—undeveloped as it was—emerges from what he wrote on the subject.

He regarded curiosity—a natural interest in mysteries and a determination to solve them—as a powerful force in our lives. "Mystery," he wrote in the August, 1940 issue of *American Magazine*, "is the hand that beckons us up out of the clay, turns today's humdrum into an adventure, lures us into tomorrow, and transforms mortals . . . into amateur detectives" (p. 164). This one-page piece was hardly a labored or significant statement, but the diction of Stout's pronouncements merits a glance. It offers an odd combination of the serious ("beckons us up out of the clay"; "lures us into tomorrow") and the trivial ("turns . . . humdrum into an adventure"; "transforms mortals . . . into amateur detectives"). The prose betrays the pressure of a serious point behind the popular-magazine style.

"We Mystery Writers Don't Kid Ourselves," in *Publisher's Weekly* in December of the same year, changes the subject but continues this mixed tone. Mystery writers, Stout begins, are the victims of literary snobbery. Through some tongue-in-cheek calculations, he arrives at what he offers as a telling fact: of the half-million characters invented in fiction since the death of Shakespeare, the best known is Sherlock Holmes. "We warn you," he threatens the writers of "serious" fiction, "it won't be long until we outnumber you, and then we'll see who gets the front page reviews" (p. 2313). This bantering tone modulates, however, when Stout moves into an explanation of the popularity of crime fiction: "The mystery story is the modern substitute for one type of old-fashioned fairy tale, the type represented by 'Jack and the Beanstalk' and 'St. George and the Dragon'"(p. 2313). Those stories pit the disruptive forces of evil against "the safe and sane organization of human life." The detective—like Jack or St. George—fights heroically for safety and sanity. People who don't like mystery stories, Stout reasons, must be anarchists. But no sooner does he offer this theory than with an "aw, shucks" shift in tone he undercuts it: his friend Lewis Garnett doesn't like mysteries, but he is no anarchist. The piece ends genially but inconclusively.

It was not until the April 2, 1949 issue of the *Saturday Review of Literature* that Stout approached his subject seriously. In a piece commissioned by Norman Cousins, which he regarded as one of his "most closely argued" essays, Stout undertook to explain the mystery story's popularity.[1] He reiterates the idea that the detective novel is a modern fairy tale, but now the story is not one of order triumphing over disorder; rather, it is one of reason triumphing over emotion. "Man insists on nothing more desperately than that his emotions are controlled by his rational processes," Stout begins (p. 7). This is a myth, of course, but we treasure it. Detective stories give us pleasure because they retell that myth. They tell "two flagrant lies: that justice is always done and that man's reason orders his affairs" (p. 34). Thus, the true hero of a detective story is reason, and the task of telling such a story well is the task of making that abstraction human. Sherlock Holmes is the great exemplar of this theory. In American detective fiction, it is Sam Spade, who in the last chapter of *The Maltese Falcon* becomes a battleground where the reason that led him to the murderer of Miles Archer struggles with his powerful passion for her. "Never," Stout concludes, "has reason more heroically told passion to go soak its head . . . " (p. 7).

In "The Mystery Novel," written for *The Writer's Book*, a 1950 publication of the Writer's Guild, Stout fixed on a point introduced but not emphasized in his *Saturday Review* essay: since the hero of a detective novel is actually reason, and since the detective embodies that human quality just as Jack or St. George stands for order and sanity in fairy tales, then "ipso facto, the detective himself (or herself) is and must be the hero. That is the central concept which must govern throughout, from the first grasping for a plot up to the last page of revelation and triumph."[2] The detective novel must center on the process by which the detective learns the identity of the villain. Any interest in other characters, in subplots, in setting—any interest which overshadows the work of reason—disqualifies a work as a detective novel. Again, Stout points to *The Maltese Falcon* for his example: "The point always to be remembered is this, that what makes it exciting is not the discovery that Brigid killed Thursby, but the fact that Sam Spade knew it—and how he found out" (p. 67). This is the classic pattern.

Thus, Rex Stout's concept of crime fiction is finally a blend of the theoretical with the practical. He sees it appealing to human curiosity, but this is only its superficial appeal. In fact, it reaches deeper within us to a myth about ourselves which we cherish: it shows reason controlling, though not eliminating, emotion. It presents an idealized view of mankind, but one which, evidently, we need to see. This victory of reason over emotion is a matter of the dynamics of an individual personality. It translates, however, into a social victory as well—the victory of sanity and reasonableness over irrationality and destruction in human society. If the detective story is successfully to affirm our faith in reason and in social order, it cannot be distracted. It must focus always on the progress of reason towards its goal. Otherwise, the unique pattern of crime fiction becomes blurred. The result, however successful as a novel, cannot be a detective novel.

The dominant themes of the Wolfe novels grow out of Stout's concept of the genre and merge into the pattern of excursion and return which gives shape to the cycle. One crucial theme for the early novels is the idea that to be a detective you must also be a psychologist. It is insight into human behavior—not the methods of criminologists or the simple expedient of brute force— that helps Wolfe to understand the motive of the murder in *Fer-de-Lance*. In *The League of Frightened Men*, Paul Chapin's fetishism explains his perplexing behavior and attitudes, clearing the way for Wolfe's exposure of a murderer. In both of these novels the pressure of overwhelming passions—revenge in one, love in another—leads to crime. Conversely, it is reason that solves them. Wolfe, immured in his brownstone and thus free of the pressure of passion, tracks the killers by psychoanalyzing them. It is a classic duel between reason and emotion, and, as Stout asserted it must, reason wins.

In *Fer-de-Lance* Wolfe is attacked in his brownstone. It is not a perfect retreat, for passion with its destructive disorder can pierce the door. Thus, at the same time that the theme of psychological motivation for crime enters the Wolfe novels it advances the cycle towards engagement and excursion. Wolfe will have to leave his sanctuary of reason sooner or later. On the other hand, the psychological theme tends to make crime seem personal, individual. The reader sees its sources in past trauma and its consequences in the death of characters. The reader also sees the reaction it provokes in the detective who brings his reason to bear on the puzzle. But in seeing this one sees mostly a closed system, a story of interacting personalities without their social context. The emphasis falls on the mind and the personality.

The second main theme of the Wolfe novels broadens this focus by shifting attention from the individual to the family. In the Wolfe novels the family represents the source of security, affection, stability, and order. It is also however the breeding ground for hate, jealousy, lust, treachery, violence, and disorder. Family dynamics provide the background to one crime after another, as a glance at some prominent titles suggests: *In the Best Families*, *The Mother Hunt*, *The Father Hunt*, *A Family Affair*. It is not enough to be a psychologist: the detective needs to be a family psychologist to solve many of the cases. In *The Red Box* the problem is a disordered, broken family. In *The Second Confession* part of the problem is a father-daughter conflict. In *A Right to Die* a perceived slight to a family brings violence. So, families can be dangerous places, but they can also be havens. The principal example of such a family is Wolfe's own—both the inhabitants of his home and his part-time helpers who like to think of themselves as members of his "professional family." The difference between Wolfe's family and the more dangerous ones in the novels is the same difference that separates Wolfe from the criminals he pursues—reason. As a professional family, a family of detectives with Wolfe as patriarch and Archie as factotum, Saul Panzer, Fred Durkin, and Orrie Cather embody reason. They appear in the novels as aides to the solution of a crime. They are minor characters, subordinated not to Wolfe and Archie but to the unmasking of murder. The family thus merely offers a more complex, because more varied, canvas on which to paint the struggle of reason with emotion. If the family setting seems ripe for outbreaks of disordering passion, the professional family is its counterpart, just as Wolfe is any given killer's counterpart. Stout has broadened his scope but stuck to his concept of the genre.

The idea of the family serves him well in one other respect. It functions as a system of order. Crime fiction dramatizes the clash between reason and emotion, but it also emphasizes the clash between order and disorder, between community and anarchy. A crime novel that emphasizes individual psychology cannot talk about social order and disorder as well as it can about private reason and passion. But the family offers a model of the human community, and where individual psychology motivates a murder its effect on what had been ordered becomes more striking. And as another family, the professional one, moves in to reorder the disordered one, the drama enacted by detective fiction takes on social significance. The Wolfe cycle, in a sense, comes of age. It also is clear that as interest centers on the family the cycle moves further towards excursion, further away from the safety and stability of Wolfe's brownstone, further towards engagement on a broadly human scale. Here the themes of the Wolfe novels intersect with the pattern of the cycle, for the themes shift outward with the movement from home to the world.

The third important theme of the Wolfe cycle is political: personal and social order can be guaranteed only by political order. This is the logical next step after the progression from the individual to the family, and Wolfe as detective finds himself taking it as early as *Too Many Cooks* and *Over My Dead Body*. Its climax comes in *The Second Confession* and *In The Best Families* where Wolfe battles both communism and corruption in the form of Zeck, but its echoes are still heard in *A Right to Die* and *A Family Affair*. The fer-de-lance in his desk drawer, the machine-gunning of his orchids, the sausage turned to tear gas—even Pierre Ducos's horrible death in the South Room—all these demonstrate the futility of limiting one's struggle for order only to one's own world. Wolfe acknowledges that futility when he disappears on Easter Sunday to begin his fight to the finish with Zeck. The increasing interest in politics as the cycle develops is another manifestation of this fact. It is no coincidence that the climax of the political theme occurs at the point in the cycle when Wolfe is farthest away from home—when he is on the west coast, contriving his trap for Zeck.

In significant fiction, themes imply values. Out of the Wolfe cycle grows a world imbued with values; indeed, the most striking thing about Wolfe as a character is his continuous and emphatic insistence on values in everything from quality of food to quality of thought. Archie, too, lives in a world of clearly defined values—as clearly defined as the routine of their household. Some of the values are comic; others reflect the themes of the Wolfe cycle, its pattern, and its roots in Rex Stout's concept of crime fiction.

The Wolfe novels value truth. Of course, both Wolfe and Archie lie routinely to the police and others in their search for murderers, but that is irrelevant. The crucial fact is that they are devoted to finding murderers, to finding out the truth. Lies committed in pursuit of that goal merely serve the truth which is their goal. But Wolfe's intellect thrives on other kinds of truth as well. He removed Sir Thomas More's *Utopia* from his bookshelves upon discovering that More had framed Richard III to flatter Henry. He despises advertising for its commitment to ignoring truth when it will not help sales. Madeline Fraser sells Hi-Spot, a soft drink, with great success, yet the taste of it makes her ill. "She is a dangerous woman," Wolfe comments. He will not permit flummery, flattery, or self-deception from clients, from victims, from Archie, or even from himself.

The Wolfe novels also value order. Wolfe's rigid daily schedule, his fondness for the routine he shares with Archie, his contempt for international intrigue and domestic corruption, but most of all his crusade to unmask the violators of social order—murderers—all these attest to his respect for order. The haphazard, the unexpected, and the unpredictable offend Wolfe not because he is small-minded but because he values the stability and security of order. It is tempting to link his value of truth with his value of order, to find a metaphysical ground where they merge, so that truth becomes order and order truth. But this is not Wolfe either. These novels value not so much a particular form of order as order in the abstract, order as opposed to destructive disorder. They value the kind of order affirmed in "Jack and the Beanstalk" and "St. George and the Dragon." They value the order that gives sense to human community and finally to civilization itself.

Finally, the Wolfe novels value reason. They dramatize the pursuit of crime by reason as embodied in Nero Wolfe. Amidst a world, like the real one, dominated by unpredictable, uncontrollable passion, Wolfe personifies reason, which controls his thought, illuminates his inquiries, brings down his game. In doing so it upholds order, hence the cycle's approval of it. Reason is not valuable strictly in itself; its value derives from its service to human organization. Yet reason is not merely utilitarian. Wolfe's rationality is hard-won. Bloodless rationality is the property of an Arnold Zeck, not a Nero Wolfe. The value of reason in this sense is that it is the product of a struggle. Upholders of order are our romantic heroes, and Wolfe qualifies under that category. His daily schedule is as much an insistence on order as a tribute to it; similarly, Wolfe's fat, his gruffness, and his seclusion betray his struggle to insulate himself from emotions, to harness them, to grant them a place, but a smaller one than they claim. Reason then is a goal; it is also a process, a struggle. The Wolfe novels value it as both.

3

Family Tensions:
The Early Novels

Fer-de-Lance, The League of Frightened Men, The Red Box, Too Many Cooks, Some Buried Caesar

Fer-de-Lance(1934)

Fer-de-Lance, the first Nero Wolfe novel and one of the best, tells a story of love, betrayal, violence, and revenge. These actions unfold in the placid country-house atmosphere of upstate New York, but the darker setting of the Argentine pampas, a frontier where behavior is free and no questions are asked, intrudes upon the peace of rural New York and finally threatens even the safety and security of the house on West Thirty-fifth Street.

The story begins with Wolfe sampling commercial beers in hopes of finding a drinkable substitute for bootleg brew. Fred Durkin interrupts, and the novel's first significant event occurs—he introduces his wife's best friend, Maria Maffei, whose brother Carlo, an itinerant metalworker, has been missing for three days. Impressed by her familial devotion but doubtful that the case will interest him, Wolfe agrees to a preliminary investigation and dispatches Archie to Carlo Maffei's rooming house.

Archie comes back not with a clue but with Anna Fiore, a servant who had heard Maffei agree to meet someone the night he disappeared. Wolfe discovers that Maffei had cut out of the newspaper an article on the death of Peter Oliver Barstow, a

24

university president who had collapsed during a golf match with his son and two neighbors, and that Anna Fiore obviously and mysteriously refuses to admit that once she saw a golf club in Maffei's room. In examining Maffei's effects, Wolfe also discovers that he had responded to a newspaper advertisement for a skilled metalworker.

The coincidences come together. Wolfe offers to bet the district attorney for the county where Barstow died that if he exhumes the body and does an autopsy he will find that Barstow had been poisoned, not the victim of a heart attack as had been reported. Events prove Wolfe correct, and now he has two murders rather than one to investigate. This is fortunate, because the members of the Barstow family who now hire Wolfe are very wealthy and because the killer's ingenuity stimulates Wolfe's genius as Maffei's disappearance had not.

The subsequent investigation reveals many things, none of them expected. Barstow, who had previously been the target of a different murder attempt, had innocently stood in the way of a poisoned dart meant for someone else. The trail leads to a husband, betrayed by his wife with his best friend in the Argentine, who killed the lovers and left his infant son playing in their blood, a clever and desperately patient attempt to avenge the wife's death, a snake, the fer-de-lance, whose poison is deadlier than any snake's except the bushmaster's, and an attempt on Wolfe's life that nearly succeeds.

Wolfe puts together a chain of events leading from Maffei's disappearance to the death of a university president on a golf course and culminating in a fiery murder-suicide. At the end, Wolfe has a fifty-thousand dollar fee, the sweet taste of revenge over the district attorney who had insulted him in a previous case, and a neatly worked out solution both to the crime and to the problem of punishing the criminal.

The League of Frightened Men (1935)

The League of Frightened Men, a story of thwarted love, obsessional longing, and sly revenge, focuses on human psychology— on the importance of being able to understand it, on the failure of psychologists, on its place in crime fiction. Above all it is a story about masks, disguises, pretenses, and the strength of the emotions which defy our attempts to cover them up.

In *Fer-de-Lance* the problem had been motive. Who would want to kill Peter Oliver Barstow and why? Not until Wolfe discovers that the dart that killed Barstow was meant for someone else and that it was sped on its way by revenge can he identify the killer. In *The League of Frightened Men* there are two sudden, violent deaths, but here everyone knows the identity of the killer and everyone knows his motive—revenge. The problem is proof. But just as everyone was wrong about Barstow's death, everyone is wrong about Paul Chapin in this book—everyone, that is, except Nero Wolfe, who shows that detection can be a literary art.

As a freshman at Harvard, Paul Chapin had been gravely injured in a hazing incident. In the years that followed, the upperclassmen responsible for his injury formed an association morbidly called the League of Atonement and dedicated to helping Chapin in every possible way. Twenty-three years after Chapin's Harvard graduation and just three years after he has achieved a measure of independence by marrying and publishing a successful novel, two members of the League die suddenly and violently. After each death the surviving members receive poetic epistles with the ominous refrain, "Ye should have killed me." They are no longer the League of Atonement but the League of Frightened Men.

Andrew Hibbard, professor of psychology at Columbia University, is the first to lose his nerve. He comes to Wolfe with a plea for protection. Wolfe, as always with such a request, refuses. A few days later Hibbard disappears. His niece tries to engage Wolfe but he, with an eye on the prospective fee, persuades the League to retain him to rid them of the fear of Chapin, of the verse warnings, and of those responsible for the deaths and disappearance of the two absent members.

Perhaps only Wolfe would begin a case involving an author by reading through his work. He also however has Chapin tailed by Fred Durkin and Orrie Cather. He instructs Saul Panzer to find the missing Hibbard, and he sets Archie on the trail of the typewritten warnings received by members of the League. They discover two facts: Chapin did send the ominous "Ye should have killed me" poems; more importantly they discover that Chapin owns a fancy leather box full of lingerie belonging to Mrs. Loring Burton, wife of one member of the League and Chapin's former fiancée, by whom Chapin's wife was formerly employed as a maid. It contains as Wolfe says, "the soul of a man."

But then Dr. Burton is murdered, Chapin arrested for the crime, and it looks as though Inspector Cramer will, for once, cheat Wolfe out of a fee. Far from seeking to pin two murders on the crippled novelist, Wolfe and Archie must exonerate him and find the real murderer. Here plain detection takes over from psychology, and before long Chapin is again in possession of his precious box, Cramer is in possession of a murderer, and Wolfe is in possession of a very large fee.

The Red Box (1937)

Like *Fer-de-Lance* and *The League of Frightened Men*, *The Red Box* tells a story about what happens in a family when the natural relationships become distorted by unnatural human vices—in this case, greed. As with *Fer-de-Lance*, the novel opens with an accidental murder. A beautiful young model eats poisoned candy and dies during a fashion show. The police can do nothing, so Llewellyn Frost, an impulsive young producer, hires Wolfe to do two things: find out where the poisoned candy came from and get his cousin, Helen Frost, also a model, away from the fashion house where she works and where the poisoning occurred. This opening is notable mainly because Wolfe must go to the fashion house himself to investigate, something he flatly refuses to do until Frost, primed by Archie, presents him with a letter signed by six leading orchid growers requesting him to undertake the case.

Almost immediately Wolfe discovers that Helen Frost's account of the poisoning, which she witnessed, is false. His discovery prompts several attempts to protect the beautiful heiress. Llewellyn Frost quickly tries, and fails, to fire Wolfe. Her employer, a harassed man named Boyden McNair whom she has known from infancy and calls "Uncle Boyd," her mother Calida

Frost, Llewellyn's father Dudley Frost, and Perren Gebert, a sardonic Frenchman who hangs about the Frosts, all try to call Wolfe off the case as well. Wolfe perseveres in questioning Helen until McNair appears with an admission and a request. He admits that he too has lied about the poisoning which opened the book, and he requests that Wolfe consent to be executor of his estate, bequeathing to him a red leather box. It is almost as if McNair expects to die soon. And he does. Moments later he collapses, convulsed, on the rug before Wolfe's desk, poisoned by two aspirin tablets he had taken from a bottle in his pocket. Wolfe is furious.

Before his horrible death McNair begins to tell the story of his life—a story that becomes as well an account of the Frost family's life in Europe before the first world war. McNair, a Scot, had been studying art and starving in Paris in 1913 when he married an American girl. At the same time, a Scots girl, Calida Buchan, also studying art, married a wealthy American, Edwin Frost, so she would not have to starve. But two years later McNair's wife died giving birth to their daughter. Edwin Frost entered the British aviation corps and died in battle in 1916. By the end of the war there was only McNair, Calida Frost, and a daughter traveling with her who was heir to the fantastic Frost fortune. McNair admits that he has hidden important information about this circle. He declares his determination never to divulge it, and dies screaming, "The red box . . . God, let me tell him."

Wolfe searches for the red box, for the truth about that circle of expatriates in Paris, and for the solution to two murders (soon to become three, for Perren Gebert too dies a hideous death by poison). In the process Helen and Llewellyn Frost both learn crucial facts about their families, a devilish murderer is brought to bay, and Wolfe manages another ending which saves him a trip to the courtroom to testify in a murder trial.

Too Many Cooks (1938)

Too Many Cooks begins with Nero Wolfe not only leaving his home but preparing to travel by train to West Virginia. The occasion is the quadrennial meeting of Les Quinze Maîtres, the fifteen masters, an elite club of the world's finest chefs, to be held at Kanawha Spa, home of the dean of Les Quinze, Louis Servan. As the guest of honor Wolfe has agreed to speak on the topic, "*Contributions Américaines à la Haute Cuisine.*" But Wolfe has another motive for this trip as well. One of the masters is Jerome Berin of the Corridona in San Remo, creator of *saucisse minuit*, a dish Wolfe hopes to prepare in the brownstone if only he can get Berin to divulge the recipe.

Wolfe first attempts to wheedle the recipe out of Berin on the train but fails, unlike Archie, who becomes friendly with Berin's beautiful daughter, Constanza. In talking to Berin, though, Wolfe and Archie hear of Phillip Laszio, another of the fifteen master chefs who, Berin declares, should and will die. Laszio presumed to serve *saucisse minuit* at the Churchill in New York, and he has offended elsewhere as well. He stole the recipe for *Rognons aux Montagnes* from a chef named Zelota; he stole Marko Vukcic's wife, Dina; he stole the position of *chef de cuisine* at the Churchill from Leon Blanc, another of Les Quinze.

Despite the tensions among Les Quinze Maîtres uncovered by this recital, the gathering goes well enough at first. The opening dinner is a triumph, and after it the fifteen prepare for a contest. Nine dishes of *sauce printemps* are set out on a table, each lacking one of the nine spices in the sauce. Each contestant must taste each dish once and name the missing spice. The excitement begins when Wolfe, who goes last, beckons Archie into the tasting room. There, on the floor behind a screen, lies Phillip Laszio, a knife in his back. After an investigation the prosecuting attorney arrests Jerome Berin, who had publicly threatened Laszio's life repeatedly. Here is Wolfe's chance to put Berin in his debt, so when Servan, Vukcic, and Constanza Berin all beg him to clear Berin he undertakes to do so but refuses a fee.

Wolfe discovers that the wife of one of the fifteen accidentally saw a black man in Kanawha Spa livery in the parlor where Laszio was killed just at the time of the murder. This puzzling information becomes crucial when, as a result of a noble speech on human rights to the black cooks and waiters of the hotel, Wolfe discovers that Paul Whipple, a young waiter, saw the same person at the same time but through another door. This strange figure also saw Whipple and put his hand to his lips to signal him not to reveal his presence there. Whipple's most startling statement, though, does not corroborate the other testimony. The man, he claims, was white, covered in burnt cork to pass as one of the staff.

These revelations secure Berin's release and his gratitude, but they nearly end Wolfe's career as well. The murderer, frightened by Wolfe's acumen, shoots at him through an open window as he is practicing his speech before the last dinner of the meeting. Only Archie's quickness saves Wolfe's life. The murderer is now doomed, for Wolfe does not take such attacks lightly. The result is a flurry of long-distance detecting, an examination of the female character, a shocking revelation, and a victory for Wolfe in two ways: his speech is an enormous success and the murderer is exposed. But there is yet another, longer-lasting reward. Under the pressure of his debt, Berin reveals his recipe for *saucisse minuit*.

Some Buried Caesar(1939)

This novel, Stout's own favorite of his works, opens with a bang— the bang of a front tire on Wolfe's car as it blows out, sending the car, with Wolfe in it, careening off the road into a tree.[1] Wolfe and Archie are en route to Crowfield to exhibit orchids at the North Atlantic Exposition, an undertaking to which Wolfe has been driven by his desire to humiliate one Charles E. Shanks who had twice refused to trade crossbreeds with Wolfe.

The immediate problem, though, is that their car is eighteen miles from Crowfield and will not be going any farther. Wolfe and Archie start to cut across a field to the nearest house to phone for assistance when they are frozen in their tracks by the sight of an enormous bull preparing to rush them. When the bull charges, Archie has agility enough to vault the fence enclosing the pasture, but Wolfe must content himself with a perch on a boulder in the middle of the field where he stands, trying to look dignified. There are three onlookers to the scene: the ineffectual hired hand who is guarding the bull; Caroline Pratt, whose uncle owns the field, the bull, and the house with the telephone; and Lily Rowan.

Wolfe and Archie are rescued and taken to Pratt's house where they find the scene if anything more tense. Thomas Pratt, a fast-food baron, has bought the bull, a champion Guernsey named Hickory Caesar Grindon, for the preposterous sum of $45,000 from Monte McMillan, a local Guernsey breeder whose herd has been nearly wiped out by anthrax, a cattle disease. Pratt's niece Caroline, his nephew Jimmy, and Lily Rowan have come up from New York for a barbecue—Hickory Caesar's. Pratt plans to butcher, cook, and serve the bull as a publicity stunt, and breeders all over the state are enraged. A more particular hostility however emanates from the neighboring Osgood family, with whom the Pratts' relations have always been bad. Clyde Osgood, son of the wealthy and arrogant Frederick Osgood, comes by to accuse Pratt of barbecuing Hickory Caesar to embarrass and annoy his father, whose herd boasts no bull the equal of the one Pratt plans to eat in a bath of publicity. Young Osgood concludes that Pratt will not barbecue Hickory Caesar at all. He bets $10,000 on that claim and stalks off.

Wolfe finds the accommodations at Pratt's home so congenial that he offers Archie as a guard for the bull, and thus it is Archie who discovers Clyde Osgood's body horribly mutilated in the field late that evening, the bull poking at it with his horns. The local authorities call it an accidental death, but Archie is mortified that anyone should die in a pasture he is guarding. To quiet him Wolfe assures him it was murder after all. Like Wolfe, Clyde's father does not believe his son's death was accidental; unlike Wolfe, he has no basis for this belief. Archie knows an opening when he sees one, and before long they have a client—Osgood—and a new place to stay—Osgood's mansion on a nearby hill.

Preliminary inquiries reveal that Clyde Osgood had lost large sums of money in pursuit of Lily Rowan and had then lost even more gambling to recoup his earlier losses. In desperation he had accepted $10,000 from a high-class crook named Bronson, in exchange for which he had promised entrée for Bronson into New York's most exclusive bridge clubs. Bronson too is on the scene, having come from New York with Clyde on this visit home. Bronson is slimy but not particularly interesting until he is found underneath a pile of straw at the exposition, a pitchfork through

his heart. The murdered Clyde had left other complications behind him as well. He and Caroline Pratt had been secretly engaged until Clyde had fallen for Lily Rowan. From this tangle
of financial, romantic, and familial complications only one thing
emerges: to have made that wager about Hickory Caesar, Clyde
Osgood must have known something about the bull that no one
else knew, something dangerous enough to motivate murder.
Further, he must have been forced to share that knowledge with
his impatient creditor, Bronson. Now both of them are dead.

Away from home, occupied with his orchid exhibit, an ob-
streperous client, and a foolish district attorney, Wolfe needs to
find out the dangerous secret about Hickory Caesar Grindon and
to connect it with the deaths of Osgood and Bronson. He has to
manufacture evidence to squeeze the truth about the bull out of
its breeder, Monte McMillan. Archie even does time in the Crowfield County Jail. The novel ends happily, though, with talk about
a wedding. It is not Archie's of course, but in Lily Rowan, whom
Mr. Osgood calls a "sex maniac," and Caroline Pratt a "vampire,"
Archie may have met his match.

ANALYSIS OF THEMES

The most striking aspect of the early Wolfe novels is their interest
in the psychology of human behavior—especially that of criminals. This was an interest Rex Stout had displayed in his early
writing for the pulps, but it flowers and develops here in ways
that were to remain important throughout the Wolfe series.[2]
Whereas in his early fiction Stout had seen psychology mainly
as a means to entrap criminals, here it becomes an integral part
of character, plot, and—most importantly—theme.

The reader of the Wolfe novels hardly ever encounters a thug.
Admittedly there is Lips Egan in *The Golden Spiders* (1953) and
Thumbs Meeker and his crowd in the short story "Before I Die"
(1949), but by and large the lower echelons of crime, the enfor-
cers and punks, have little place in this world. Nor are there many
professional criminals from the higher echelons of crime—the
notable exception being Arnold Zeck. Instead the criminals in
these novels are usually more or less normal people from upper
and upper-middle class backgrounds who have been pushed into

crime by some overwhelming, often emotional, pressure. This pressure might be vengeance, jealousy, fear, lust—emotions which everyone feels but which in these cases become secret, corrosive passions. This is the reason the Wolfe of these early novels is more a psychologist than a detective, more a man of arts and letters than a policeman; he deals not with the hardened criminals that populate hard-boiled crime fiction but rather with the obsessive, repressive types in whom common emotions have become just strong enough to tip the precarious balance between their acquired social and their instinctive anti-social behavior in favor of the latter. The result, by society's definition, is a criminal.

Wolfe reminds anyone who will listen that he is an artist, not a scientist. A scientist can analyze a bloodstain; a technician can identify a tire print; but only an artist can read a man's soul in his books or wheedle his life story out of him over a glass of beer and know the springs of his behavior. A few examples will quickly show the important role psychology plays in these books.

Fer-de-Lance emphasizes the "family secret" of the Barstows—that Mrs. Barstow, whose emotional equilibrium is a fragile thing, has had a series of breakdowns culminating in an attempt to shoot her husband. His accidental murder accomplishes her cure. Moreover E. D. Kimball, whose hearty energy masks his terrible unhappiness, discovered his Argentine wife in adultery and murdered her before their child, who sat playing on the floor. The unraveling of the plot depends in part on the effect of this trauma on young Manuel. Finally the novel provides a running commentary on psychology. Ellen Barstow tells Archie, "I think we would be better off without modern psychology, everything it tells us is so ugly," and Wolfe, as part of his effort to get the caddies to help him understand Barstow's murder, tells a story of a meeting of a hundred psychologists, all of whom saw a murder acted out before their eyes and all of whom reported the event differently.[3] Archie explains, "he had given them the feeling that he was counting on them to help him show how dumb the hundred psychologists had been . . . " (p.185).

In *The League of Frightened Men* one of the main characters, Andrew Hibbard, is a psychologist who disguises himself and starts following Paul Chapin out of fear that he is next on Chapin's

murder list. In doing so he learns a lesson not so much about
Chapin as about psychology:

> In these eleven days I have learned that psychology, as a formal
> science, is pure hocus-pocus. All written and printed words,
> aside from their function of relieving boredom, are meaningless
> drivel. I have fed a half-starved child with my own hands. I have
> seen two men batter each other with their fists until the blood
> ran. I have watched boys picking up girls. I have heard a woman
> tell a man, in public and with a personal application, facts which
> I had dimly supposed were known, academically, only to those
> who have read Havelock Ellis. . . . It is utterly amazing, I tell
> you, how people do things they happen to feel like doing. And
> I have been an instructor in psychology for seventeen years!
> *Merde!*[4]

Yet despite Hibbard's attack on the academic discipline of psychology, this novel is built around a case of fetishism. Paul
Chapin is consistently described in the book as twisted and
warped, and crippled both physically and mentally. It is the "bitter torment in the romantic cripple's heart," to use Wolfe's
phrase, that causes most of the novel's confusion by spurring
Chapin to pretend to have murdered members of the League.
Wolfe's perception that in his novels Chapin repeatedly kills his
former classmates leads him to conclude that Chapin could not
be the murderer: "I had merely read his books; but I was aware
. . . that Chapin could not possibly commit a pre-meditated murder. . . . And you, Mr. Hibbard, a psychologist!" (p.288).

In *The Red Box* the allusions to psychology continue. After
Boyden McNair has been murdered by proxy right in Wolfe's
office, Archie is typically itching to go after the mysterious red
box mentioned in his will. Wolfe, also typically, will not satisfy
him by sending him on that futile errand, so Archie turns sar-
castic:

> If I was the kind of man you are, I would just sit calmly in my
> chair with my eyes shut, and use psychology on it. Like you did
> with Paul Chapin, remember? First I would decide what the
> psychology of McNair was like, covering every point. Then I
> would say to myself, if my psychology was like that, and if I had
> a very important article like a red box to hide, where would I
> hide it?[5]

A pattern has already been established. Wolfe is a psychologist, labeled as such by Archie. These are novels of detection, but they focus on the complex of emotion and circumstance that provokes action as much as on the action itself. Under these circumstances, it is surprising to hear Wolfe, when asked, "Do you go in for psychology?" responding first by choking and then with a firm, "No" (*Some Buried Caesar*, p. 37). But it is not psychology per se that Wolfe rejects; it is academic psychology of the Andrew Hibbard kind. Wolfe is a psychologist because he is a humanist. His is the attitude of Terence, the Roman playwright, who had one of his characters proclaim, "I am a man; nothing human is foreign to me."

If Wolfe is a psychologist, he needs material to study, and these early novels supply it, for all of them center on family dynamics. The crimes committed here grow out of the emotions and circumstances bred in families. The reader of the early Wolfe novels finds himself embroiled in parent-and-child as well as husband-and-wife battles in which marriage, independence from the family, and other developmental crises become the backdrop for crime.

The plot of *Fer-de-Lance*, Oedipal in its outlines, centers on a father-mother-son triangle as the cause of at least five deaths. In *The League of Frightened Men* the problem is not, strictly speaking, a family one, but in some ways it is. Chapin marries a woman who can supply him with intimate clothing belonging to his true love. Of course Paul Chapin's activities actually mask those of the real murderer, whose motive is more banal, but the weight of the novel falls on Chapin and his distorted family life. In *The Red Box* a daughter does not know either her true father or her true mother. In the end, entire family relationships must be sorted out and reconstructed to eliminate both the murderer and the ill-will she has caused from the new family circle that forms at the novel's conclusion. In *Too Many Cooks* the emphasis shifts back from parent-child to husband-wife relationships. The novel is littered with broken marriages, broken courtships, and discussions of marriage. At least one of these marriages is sufficiently weak to give rise to a murder and to draw in suspects from among the other weakened families in the novel. Finally

Some Buried Caesar offers, as if to conclude and summarize these themes, parent-child tensions, husband-wife tensions, and tensions among young lovers that provide the background to a series of murders in the pastoral setting of a local fair. In these early novels, with their interest in human behavior and its springs, the family is not a bulwark against but a crucible for jealousy, vengeance, hatred, deception, and sometimes love. It would take a psychologist rather than a policeman or lawyer to investigate anything here.

The Red Box provides a specific example. It opens with Wolfe being badgered into taking a case by Llewellyn Frost, a young producer concerned about the safety of Helen Frost, a relative whom he describes with the surprising label, "My ortho-cousin, the daughter of my father's brother" (p.9). Instantly, the plot veers towards family tension. Wolfe astutely inquires, "Indeed. . . . Are you an anthropologist?", for only an anthropologist could be expected to know the difference between ortho-cousins and cross-cousins. Cross-cousins are allowed to marry in some cultures but not ortho-cousins. Obviously Frost loves Helen and has gone to great trouble to find a way around the taboo that stands between him and his resolve. The situation only becomes further complicated when the reader learns that Helen Frost works as a model at the firm owned by Boyden McNair, apparently no relation but whom she nevertheless calls "uncle." Her mother, Calida Frost, is related to Llewellyn's father, Dudley, only by marriage, having married Dudley's brother before the war in which he was killed. To confuse matters more, McNair had lost a daughter approximately the age of Helen Frost at that same period and, in a display of loyalty to the dead that Wolfe calls "ghoulish," McNair asks Helen Frost to spend the day in seclusion with him each year on the anniversary of his daughter's birthday. The consequence of this, as every reader of the novel knows, is that any conversation involving the Frosts becomes a tangle of "brother-in-laws" and "sister-in-laws," as though to emphasize linguistically the odd web of relations that holds this group together.

Of course the other link between these people is their apparent involvement in a murder. One of the models with whom Helen Frost works has died from poisoning, and Helen is apparently withholding information. Llewellyn as her cousin, his father as her trustee, Calida Frost as her mother, and McNair as her "uncle," all wish to prevent Helen from being questioned. Since Wolfe is committed, the attempts fail, and the result is a revelation that totally restructures the families. Calida Frost is not Helen Frost's mother, nor is Llewellyn any longer her ortho-cousin. Her true name is Glenna McNair and her uncle turns out to be her father. As in a Shakespearean comedy there is a found-ing of a new order at the end—a new child-parent axis forms, the incest taboo is removed for Glenna and Llewellyn, and a murderer is removed from society.

Some Buried Caesar, which depicts both interfamily and in-trafamily tension, offers another good example of the early in-terest in family dynamics. The Pratts and the Osgoods—the new rich and the old money—do not live on good terms. Mrs. Osgood was engaged to Mr. Pratt at one time, until Osgood carried her away. Similarly Jimmy Pratt and Nancy Osgood were "really friendly," as were Clyde Osgood and Caroline Pratt, until Clyde Osgood's attention was diverted to Lily Rowan. In fact Clyde and Caroline were privately engaged before Clyde met Lily and, as Archie puts it, "the Osgood-Pratt axis got multiple fracture."[6] But the novel focuses on inter rather than intrafamily tension. Neither Pratt nor Osgood gets on well with his younger relation. To Pratt, Jimmy is "My only nephew, and no good for anything at all" (p. 26). Osgood and his son quarreled at their last meeting. Clyde had spent large sums futilely courting Lily Rowan and, his money gone, took to gambling. He was $10,000 in debt and had come to ask for help. According to Osgood: "I was in a tem-per, and that roused his, and he started to walk out. I accused him of betraying me, . . .Then he did walk out" (p. 125). At the time of Clyde's death he and his father were not on speaking terms.

In both cases the mother is either dead or negligible—dead in Pratt's case and negligible in Osgood's—and the closest re-placement is a sister. But sisters cannot often patch father-son quarrels, and they do not here. One also has to assume, though the novel is not specific on this point, that there is also brother-sister tension in both families. After all, when Nancy Osgood became involved with Jimmy Pratt, Clyde became involved with

Caroline, and it was the breakup of the second pair that led to
the breakup of the first. Surely somewhere Jimmy resented Caroline's part in this, and Nancy Clyde's, though of course it is Lily
who comes in for most of the resentment from both couples.
Again, a tangled web of jealousy and intrigue provides the background for Wolfe's investigation. And even though he is not
called upon to exercise his insight on the Pratt-Osgood axis, it is
this element of the plot that provides the link with the other early
novels.

But there is yet another family—the first family of the Wolfe
novels—that requires discussion. They live at West Thirty-fifth
Street. In the Wolfe novels—especially in the early ones which
see the family as a crucible of dangerous emotions—Wolfe and
Archie as a family unit supply the comic analogue to the difficult
and dangerous families that populate the novels. The atmosphere
in the brownstone is often as tense as the atmosphere in the
McNair, Pratt, and Osgood families. Sexual jealousy does not
disturb the Wolfe-Archie relationship, but professional jealousy
can. So can pride of other sorts—sartorial, gustatory, and so on.
One might expect, too, that Wolfe and Archie might clash at the
rough edges where their personalities do not fit. This is just what
happens.
    The main source of tension of course is the intellectual dis-
parity between Wolfe and Archie. Wolfe has a feeling for phenomena, Archie merely a feeling for facts. Thus when Wolfe
sends Archie over to Carlo Maffei's room to investigate he instructs, "returning here bring with you any articles that seem to
you unimportant." Archie's aside hints at tensions despite his
disclaimer: "I thought it was unnecessary for him to take a dig
at me before a stranger, but I had long since learned that there
was no point in resenting his pleasantries" (p. 13). This notion—
that to Wolfe Archie seems slow-witted and that to Archie Wolfe
seems conceited—becomes a steady theme running throughout
the Wolfe novels. Sometimes it becomes a valuable index to other
sorts of tensions between the two that mirror tensions set up in
the families in the novels. Wolfe and Archie do not have to struggle with sexual jealousy in an ordinary way because of Wolfe's
gynephobia, but a comic form of that tension always underlies

the action. There is the possibility that Archie will, with all his
philandering, find a woman to marry and thus destroy the family
he has made with Wolfe. Thus in *Fer-de-Lance* when Archie is
badgering Wolfe for an errand he provokes this tart comment:
"Some day, Archie, you will have to marry a woman of very mod-
est mental capacity to get an appropriate audience for your
wretched sarcasms" (p. 60). Here the sexual jealousy, normally
repressed in the Wolfe-Archie family, is transferred to the more
familiar context of Wolfe's attacks on Archie's intellect, producing a doubly sharp attack.

Archie on the other hand has his objections to Wolfe. They
are mixed with admiration and tempered by it, just as Wolfe's
attacks on Archie are tempered by his affection for him and respect for his competence as a man of action; nevertheless, Archie
makes no serious attempt to hide his feelings. For Archie, Wolfe's
most objectionable quality is his conceit. That is why one of Archie's favorite roles is that of deflator. For Archie, this role is
part of his directness, his preference for facts over phenomena,
for pictures over ideas. It leads to the attitude that lies behind
Archie's descriptions of Wolfe as an "actor" and to his characterization of Wolfe's concluding performances as "charades."

At the end of *The League of Frightened Men* Paul Chapin
informs Wolfe that he will be in Chapin's next book, where he
will die violently. After Chapin leaves this exchange occurs:

> I said to Wolfe: "I had intended to go to a movie after lunch, but
> now I can't. I've got work ahead. I've got to figure out certain
> suggestions to make to Paul Chapin for his next book. My head
> is full of ideas."
> "Indeed." Wolfe's bulk came forward to permit him to ring
> for beer. "Archie." He nodded at me gravely. "Your head full of
> ideas? Even my death by violence is not too high a price to pay
> for so rare and happy a phenomenon as that." (p. 308)

This exchange shows the playful sparring of Wolfe and Archie
in another light—the light in which family tension appears in
these early novels—as a source of potential violence. Here it is
Archie finding a suitably ironic outlet for repressed violent urges
towards Wolfe, the father figure. Of course in the final analysis
the overall effect of this scene is comic. The death threats of both
Chapin and Archie are harmless, for Chapin is ineffectual while

Archie is not serious. Even Stout's pun—on "gravely"—though it has a dark side, is mainly comic, as are all of the other similar scenes in these novels. It is their function to be comic; they counterpoint the scenes of family tension and violence in the early novels which are not comic. In parodying those scenes they offer both continuity with the action of the novels and change by putting family violence in perspective, framing it with a vision of family tensions corrected by comedy and made to dissipate in larger visions of unity.

This then is the world of the early Wolfe novels, a violent world—for Wolfe and Archie making their living by violence. Rex Stout portrays a world dominated by personalities, one in which the detective is a psychologist and one in which the family replaces the mean streets of the hard-boiled novel as the arena for crime. The criminals here are the passions—jealousy, hate, love, greed—and they are sinister indeed. Only in the comic family on West Thirty-fifth Street do we see them in perspective.

4

The Problem of Politics: The Middle Novels

Over My Dead Body, Too Many Women, And Be A Villain, The Second Confession, In the Best Families, Before Midnight

Over My Dead Body (1940)

In *Over My Dead Body* the Nero Wolfe novels expand their focus to include politics, the major concern of the series in its middle period. But the family interest is not abandoned. Families and politics merge in these middle novels, and the family comes to seem a bulwark against threatening forces from the world of politics.

The book opens with a Montenegrin woman, Carla Lovchen, calling upon Wolfe. Miss Lovchen and a friend, Neya Tormic, teach fencing at the Milton academy in New York and Miss Tormic is in trouble. She has been accused by a customer of stealing a valuable box of diamonds from his clothes in his locker during a fencing lesson, and the two women have come to appeal for Wolfe's help—not because they are his compatriots but for an even more pressing reason. Neya Tormic claims to be Wolfe's daughter.

It turns out that Wolfe did indeed adopt an orphaned three-year-old girl in a fit of romantic exuberance during his loyalist days in Montenegro, but having left her in good hands when he came to America, he had heard nothing of her since. Archie goes to the fencing academy and investigates the charge, but three events happen so quickly while he is there that the situation becomes stickier, not cleaner: the indignant fencing student finds his diamonds safe elsewhere; another student—Percy Ludlow—is brutally murdered with a fencing sword equipped with a sharp tip called a *col de mort*; and Archie finds the blood-stained *col de mort* in his pocket and has to flee the scene before he is searched.

Meanwhile Wolfe and Archie discover that on her first visit Carla Lovchen hid a paper in a book on Wolfe's shelves. It is a note from the Balkan prince Stefan Donevitch empowering his wife Vladanka to act for him in the matter of Bosnian forest concessions. When it turns out that the murdered Ludlow was a British agent and that another fencing student, Rudolph Faber, is an agent of Nazi Germany, it becomes clear that this is a case not simply of murder but of international intrigue, which Wolfe calls the "dirtiest" of all the activities of humankind.

Donald Barrett, a wealthy young American of the international firm of Barrett and De Russy, has befriended the Montenegrin women. Neither of the women will be candid about their business in the country, and Barrett complicates matters further by butting in with offers to buy Wolfe's silence and, worse, by spiriting away a witness Wolfe wants to speak to. She is a designer named Madame Zorka, who claims to have seen Miss Tormic put the *col de mort* in Archie's coat pocket just before the police arrived. Archie finally tracks Madame Zorka to her hideout and brings her to Wolfe, but she escapes from the south room by climbing out the window and down the fire escape.

Things have reached this impasse—Ludlow is dead; a woman claiming to be Wolfe's adopted daughter is embroiled in some sort of intrigue involving Balkan royalty, Bosnian forest concessions, and an international financial firm; and the city is littered with foreign agents—when the situation is further complicated by another murder. This time it is Faber, the German agent, stabbed to death in the apartment rented to Miss Lovchen and Miss Tormic. Wolfe is fed up at his involvement in a business he regards on principle as sordid and with a client who may or may not be his daughter and who, worst of all, cannot pay a fee. It is a family obligation however. Only by luck and tenacity does Wolfe bring the murderer to justice. Even then he faces death in his office at the hands of a young woman whose last words to him are, "Over my dead body."

Too Many Women (1947)

Too Many Women is Archie's novel. Of course the peculiar talents of Wolfe entrap the criminal here, but overall he plays a small role in the novel. Archie does nearly all the investigating; that is not in itself new, but the twist here is that his headquarters is not the house on West Thirty-fifth Street but the offices of Naylor-Kerr, Inc., an engineering firm.

The novel begins with Wolfe and Archie at odds, undergoing what Archie calls a "coolness." Both Archie and Wolfe are eager to be out of each other's way for a few days, so when Jasper Pine, the president of Naylor-Kerr, wants to hire Wolfe to investigate the death of an employee, Wolfe arranges for Archie to take a job with the firm as a personnel consultant, a job which will require him to spend eight hours a day away from the brownstone.

The problems at Naylor-Kerr began when Pine noticed that the turnover rate for clerical employees of the firm was over twenty-eight percent for the previous year—too high. Pine sent a questionnaire to all section heads, one for each employee who had left the company, asking for an explanation of the departure. The results were more than he bargained for. The section head of the stock department reported that one of his employees, a Waldo Wilmot Moore, had been murdered.

The police knew of Moore's death, but it had been ruled a hit-and-run. Murder, however, requires malice aforethought, and with the stock department section head, Mr. Kerr Naylor, the bizarre son of one of the firm's two founders and Pine's brother-in-law, refusing to supply details, the company has no choice but to turn to Wolfe. Gossip over the report has reached the point where it constitutes a morale problem.

Beginning work under the pseudonym of Peter Truett, Archie discovers that the stock department is full of beautiful young stenographers and happily observes that he is being paid to question them all. His only worry is Kerr Naylor, who immediately exposes Archie's real identity and then further complicates his job by publicly announcing that he not only knows that Moore was murdered but also knows who did it; lacking evidence, however, he refuses to name the name. Archie, aggravated by Naylor's cat-and-mouse game and further soured on him because he is a health-food nut, would love to strangle him, but he never gets the chance, for two days later Naylor is killed in the same way and in the same spot as Moore.

Another complicating factor is Jasper Pine's wife, Cecily. She adopts young men and wants to adopt Archie. She also wants Wolfe off the case and tries to bribe him to keep whatever he finds secret. With her divided loyalties, Cecily Pine's role is ambiguous. Is she protecting her husband? Her brother? The memory of Moore, who had been her lover? Herself?

But perhaps the greatest complication of all is the tangled network of jealousies, loves, and hatreds in the stock department of Naylor-Kerr, Inc. Hester Livsey was engaged to Moore when he was suddenly killed, and Wolfe catches her in a direct lie about her relationship with Kerr Naylor. Sumner Hoff, an advisor to the stock department and an admirer from afar, insists on protecting her. Gwynne Ferris, whose involvement with Moore had inspired hatred between her and Hester Livsey, is being protected by the flaky Benjamin Frenkel, the intense assistant section head. Rosa Bendini was another of Moore's flames whose husband had punched Moore when he saw him getting out of a cab with Rosa. All these intrigues get further complicated by a gossip network which moves nearly as fast as the events themselves, inflaming and distorting everything that happens.

The result of all these complications is a case in which even Wolfe admits to being stymied. He has no clues at all. So he manufacturers one. The murderer is discovered, the ends of justice are served, and Wolfe and Archie patch up their quarrel.

And Be A Villain (1948)

And Be A Villain brings the archenemy Arnold Zeck into the Wolfe series, and in doing so adds a new kind of tension to Wolfe's family. Subject already to inner tensions that threaten, if only comically, to break it up, the family on West Thirty-fifth Street now faces a threat from outside as well. Together with the two following novels, *The Second Confession* and *In the Best Families*, *And Be A Villain* constitutes the high point of Stout's writing in his middle years.

Wolfe engages to find the murderer of Cyril Orchard, publisher of a horse-racing tip sheet who was dramatically poisoned in the middle of a guest appearance on a radio program. The program, hosted by Madeline Fraser and sponsored by the Hi-Spot bottling company, includes a segment where everyone on the program drinks a glass of Hi-Spot and praises the taste; on the day of Orchard's appearance, however, the guest went into convulsions after drinking his Hi-Spot and died horribly, gagging into the microphone.

The suspects are Madeline Fraser and Bill Meadows, her associate on the program and straight man; Elinor Vance, her researcher and scriptwriter; Deborah Koppel, her friend and producer; F. O. Savarese, a mathematics professor who was also a guest that day; Nancylee Shepherd, a pesky adolescent who idolizes Fraser; Nathan Traub, account executive at the ad agency that handles three of Fraser's sponsors; and Tully Strong, secretary of the council of sponsors for Fraser's program. Each of these people was present the day of the program, and none has a satisfactory alibi.

Wolfe, who actually seeks out this case because he needs ready cash to pay his federal income tax, succeeds in persuading Madeline Fraser and her sponsors to hire him to investigate Orchard's murder as a publicity stunt, but he is not able to secure their cooperation. This is one of those cases in which the clients withhold vital evidence because they would rather preserve various personal and professional secrets than see the murderer caught. One secret they cannot withhold is that Madeline Fraser's husband, the brother of her girlhood friend and producer

Deborah Koppel, had died of cyanide poisoning just as Orchard did. That death was ruled a suicide however and there appeared to be no question about it.

One other secret they do try to withhold. Madeline Fraser cannot drink Hi-Spot because it gives her violent indigestion. Each day on the program she drinks a specially prepared bottle of iced coffee which is made to look like Hi-Spot but is distinguished by a thin piece of scotch tape around the neck. Cyril Orchard drank from this bottle by accident; thus it appears that Madeline Fraser, not Orchard, was the intended target of the poison, but no one associated with the program can tell either Wolfe or the police this vital fact for fear of the public ridicule to which the show would be exposed if the truth about Madeline Fraser and Hi-Spot became public.

Wolfe learns this fact despite the cover-up, but it brings him no closer to solving the Orchard crime, for no one can be found who has a motive to kill Madeline Fraser. Then Beulah Poole, publisher of a tip sheet on the economy, is murdered in her office, and Wolfe's curiosity is aroused. He discovers that both Poole and Orchard were members of a brilliantly successful blackmail scheme and that their subscribers were buying not their information but their silence. Suddenly it becomes suspiciously clear that Orchard was the intended victim of the cyanide after all, and the question becomes who on the Fraser program is vulnerable to blackmail and who would kill with such maniacal steadiness.

Wolfe learns who the killer is, but not before an unheard-of event occurs. As he is investigating the background of Beulah Poole, a voice on the telephone orders him off the case. Naturally Wolfe refuses, adding insult to injury by informing the voice that he knows its owner—Arnold Zeck, friend of Congressmen, city benefactor, prominent citizen of Westchester county. Zeck is displeased; so is Wolfe. At the close of *And Be A Villain* he vows that if he must fight Zeck he will have to leave home, to disrupt the family. Both he and Archie hope it will never happen.

The Second Confession (1949)

Despite Wolfe's hope that Zeck's path will never cross his again, the two bump into each other immediately in the next Wolfe novel, *The Second Confession*. This second confrontation is even more disturbing than the first, partly because it is more dramatic, but also because it follows so closely on the heels of the Orchard case. Wolfe and Zeck both work with crime; it is clear they cannot avoid each other. Something has to give.

The Second Confession begins with the problem of Communism. James U. Sperling, wealthy mine owner, fears that his daughter Gwen has fallen in love with a Communist—Louis Rony, a young trial lawyer who is acquiring notoriety by defending criminals successfully. Since Gwen despises Communism as much as he does, Sperling simply wants Wolfe to find evidence that Rony is a Communist, thinking that will solve the problem. Wolfe however suggests defining the task more precisely: his job is to persuade Gwen to stop seeing Rony, whether by demonstrating that he is a Communist or by some other means. Sperling agrees, and Archie goes off to Stony Acres, the Sperling summer place, with instructions to captivate Gwen's heart.

While Archie is gone, Zeck calls Wolfe, instructing him immediately to stop investigating Rony. Wolfe refuses. Archie meanwhile meets Rony, discovers that he is guarding some small object kept always on his person, and determines to see it. He drugs a highball and gives it to Rony as everyone is having a drink before bedtime. But Rony pours his drink out in the ice bucket while Archie, who had switched glasses with him, discovers that someone else had drugged a highball for Rony. In making the switch Archie had merely traded one doped drink for another. In the morning Rony is lucid while Archie can barely function.

Both pride and curiosity piqued, Archie determines to satisfy both. He offers Rony a ride back to New York, arranging for them to be robbed by Saul Panzer. The object that Rony had been guarding was a Communist Party card in the name of William Reynolds. But this raises, rather than solves, problems. Is Rony Reynolds? If not, what is the nature of his interest in politics? What is his connection with Zeck? The latter question gets answered first, for as Archie, home from his weekend, reports on his adventures to Wolfe, someone machine-guns Wolfe's orchids, shattering the rooftop greenhouse, destroying hundreds of beautiful plants, and nearly killing Theodore Horstman, the gardener who lives up there.

Clearly Rony is a Zeck lieutenant. Wolfe goes to Stony Acres, enraged but outwardly calm, to confront Gwen Sperling. Whatever his politics, Rony is morally despicable because he works for Zeck, whose operations Wolfe sketches briefly. Gwen has a choice: she can drop Rony at once on the strength of the orchid massacre, or she can require solid proof of Rony's complicity, which would require a massive commitment of her father's money and Wolfe's energies in an all-out battle with Zeck. Gwen promises to decide by bedtime.

All this is clear until Archie finds Rony's body, run over by a car, in the bushes of the estate. Anxious to avoid the impudent publicity of a murder investigation, Sperling persuades his employee Webster Kane to sign a confession that satisfies the local authorities, but Wolfe immediately recognizes it as a fraud. Sperling had hired him to investigate Rony's death to prevent any of the truth about Gwen's relationship with him from getting into the papers or to the police. Since Wolfe cannot accept what he knows is a false conclusion, he continues the investigation against Sperling's orders and without his approval. Its only bright spot is that now Zeck approves; in fact, he sends Wolfe enough money to pay for the damage to the orchids. But the problem remains: how long can such amity last?

In the Best Families (1950)

The final novel in the Zeck trilogy begins with a rich, ugly, neurotic woman visiting Wolfe's office. Mrs. Barry Rackham wants to know the source of her young, handsome husband's income. She had been in the habit of giving him money whenever he needed it, but as his requests became increasingly frequent and exorbitant, she began to refuse him. Despite this fact he continues to spend money lavishly. Wolfe hates family disputes, but having just paid his taxes he needs the money, so he takes the case.

Later—on the same day Archie is scheduled to go to Birchvale, Mrs. Rackham's summer home, to get a look at Rackham—

Wolfe receives a package of Darst's sausage, his favorite kind. But instead of sausage, the package contains tear gas; if it had contained a bomb there would have been, as Archie glumly observes, sausage "not for us, but of us." The brownstone is airing out when Zeck calls with one short message: lay off Rackham. Wolfe hangs up on him.

Of course Wolfe will not give up the case. Archie goes to Birchvale anyway, armed with the likely assumption that Rackham's source of income is Zeck himself. He meets Rackham; Annabel Frey, beautiful widowed daughter-in-law of Mrs. Rackham; Lina Darrow, Mrs. Rackham's secretary; and others. He also encounters a frustrating, confusing situation: his first evening there Mrs. Rackham is stabbed to death in the woods by her house as she walks her dog. Archie and Calvin Leeds, Mrs. Rackham's cousin, neighbor, and confidant, discover the body, and when Leeds goes to call the police, Archie calls Wolfe. Flabbergasted and annoyed, Wolfe instructs him to tell the police everything except Zeck's message and his means of delivering it.

After the obligatory interviews and questions, Archie, sent away by the police with instructions to be available the next day, races back to New York, but at West Thirty-fifth Street he finds the front door wide open, Fritz and Theodore in a daze, and Wolfe gone without a trace. No one believes of course that Archie does not know Wolfe's whereabouts—in fact, the Westchester police lock him up overnight as a material witness—but it is true: Wolfe is gone, the family is broken up, and Archie is alone.

Naturally it takes a while to get over Wolfe's disappearance, but Archie finally does so. He opens his own detective office, and soon he is making more on his own than Wolfe had been paying him. He even arranges to visit Norway with Lily Rowan. Then Archie is contacted by one of Zeck's minions. Max Christie, whom he met in the Westchester jail, wants to hire Archie to tail Barry Rackham for Zeck. Then Archie meets a new man in the Zeck organization—Pete Roeder—an ugly, short-tempered man with a beard, pleated skin, and a nasal voice. Archie and Roeder work together until Archie has become part of Zeck's network, and the stage is set for the battle to the death.

Before Midnight (1955)

Lippert, Buff and Assa, a New York advertising firm, is sponsoring a contest to promote "Pour Amour" perfume, whose maker, Heery products, is one of LBA's largest accounts. The contest is spectacular, with a million dollars in prizes, including a grand prize of five hundred thousand dollars. Every week the agency publishes a four-line verse description of a woman whom history records as having used cosmetics. Using the clues in the description, contestants need only to name the woman.

It may seem unthinkable that Nero Wolfe would become engaged in a perfume contest, but this is precisely what happens. He has not entered; rather, LBA comes to him in a panic, hoping he can save their contest. After the first twenty descriptions had been published, only seventy-two contestants out of two million had identified all the women correctly. Each of these seventy-two received five more descriptions to do in a week, and at the end of that period only five contestants had answered them all correctly. LBA brought them all to New York, giving them five more verses and a week to solve them. Here a crisis occurs. Louis Dahlman, the advertising genius who conceived the contest and the descriptions, foolishly showed the five remaining contestants a sheet of paper which he claimed contained the answers to the final set of descriptions they had just been given. Later that night Dahlman was murdered, and when his body was discovered the next day the answers were gone. LBA, the integrity of its contest jeopardized, wants Wolfe to find out who took the verses out of Dahlman's wallet; he must find and name the culprit before midnight on April twentieth, the contest deadline.

The obvious suspects are the five remaining contestants—a history professor, a housewife, a researcher for a magazine, a retired adding machine salesman, and the head of a women's organization that campaigns against cosmetics. There are also Lippert, Buff, and Assa, each of whom had been somewhat eclipsed by Dahlman's rise and each of whom stood to lose power and prestige when Dahlman would become a senior partner, as he inevitably must within a year. Wolfe's problem is that Dahlman's colleagues have nothing to offer, while the contestants are too driven by the competition to help. The case flounders and Archie fumes while Wolfe reads— until two dramatic events occur in rapid succession: each of the contestants receives an anonymous letter giving the answers to the five questions everyone is working on; and one of the partners at LBA is poisoned in Wolfe's office on the very evening of the afternoon he has tried to persuade Wolfe to drop the inquiry. In his pocket is Dahlman's wallet. Enraged at the insult of a murder in his home and stung by the daring of the murderer, Wolfe acts quickly. His manner of unmasking the killer is as surprising as the criminal's identity. Archie is among the most surprised of all, and he does not like that.

ANALYSIS OF THEMES

The middle novels of the Wolfe series turn from psychology to politics. Wolfe and Archie no longer find themselves confronting bizarre personalities like Paul Chapin's or quasi-Oedipal situations like Manuel Kimball's. Instead they face international intrigue, the threat of Communism at home, and the problem of political corruption due to organized crime. No longer must Wolfe be a psychologist to trap criminals; now he must be Machiavellian, consorting with traitors, criminals, masked revolutionaries. No doubt the shift of interest from psychology to politics during the forties and fifties occurred in response to world events—the pressure of a world war and the subsequent international realignment causing the Wolfe series to turn outward rather than inward; but this shift occurred also, one suspects, in response to the increasingly claustrophobic atmosphere created by the family tension and domestic violence in the early novels. We see more of Wolfe and Archie separated and alone in the middle novels, and when they are together it appears that their relationship has matured, or at least mellowed, because there is less emphasis on the tensions between them and more on their partnership and family solidarity.

The shift to politics as a theme occurs suddenly in *Over My Dead Body*, the novel which, paradoxically, announces the most star-

tling family news of the series—that Wolfe has a daughter. Actually the coincidence of these two themes is fortuitous because
by introducing a daughter who is also mixed up in international
intrigue Stout can make the transition from one theme to the other
gracefully. When the reader hears that Wolfe's daughter from
Montenegro is in New York he is not surprised, considering the
interest of the series thus far; when he sees that she is part of an
international scramble for a document, the shock of that novelty
is tempered by the familiar. There is even a suggestion that politics and family are subtly linked. Perhaps the best emblem of
Wolfe's problematic attitude towards Montenegro, his boyhood
home, is this piece of multilingual exegesis by Archie of Wolfe's
daughter's name—Carla Lovchen: "She seems to be named after
a mountain. The Black Mountain. Mount Lovchen. Tsernagora.
Montenegro, which is the Venetian variant of Monte Nero, and
your name is Nero."[1] Wolfe's adopted daughter is the walking,
feminine symbol of his homeland; he is a son of Montenegro,
and Montenegro is his adopted daughter. Blood and politics do
mix—inevitably—and the step from one to the other is, if not
inevitable, at least natural.

Perhaps as surprising as the introduction of politics into the
series is Wolfe's bitter contempt of it—at least of international
espionage. Speaking of his early days in the Montenegrin army
and the political beliefs that prompted him to join up, Wolfe
recalls, "I then believed that all misguided or cruel people
should be shot, and I shot some" (p. 14). Wolfe retains some
political idealism, for we learn on the next page that he contributes both to Spanish loyalists and to Yugoslavian rebels, but he
scorns at least some of the kinds of behavior that political idealism produces. "Of all the activities of man," he declares, "international intrigue is the dirtiest" (p. 21). Similarly Wolfe looks
back harshly on his own espionage: "I did some work for the
Austrian government when I was too young to know better" (p.
134). But his final comment on that experience seems to be this:

> I used to be idiotically romantic. I still am, but I've got it in hand.
> I thought it romantic, when I was a boy, twenty-five years ago,
> to be a secret agent of the Austrian government. My progress
> toward maturity got interrupted by the World War and my ex-
> perience with it. (p. 134)

Politics impels people toward naive, immature, and even morally empty behavior. Wolfe can afford the luxury of his political idealism only by taxing the political behavior of himself and others. These attitudes intensify when the subject is Communism, a political theory which both Wolfe and Archie reject not only on the level of direct political activity, from espionage to campaigning for votes, but also on the level of theory. When James U. Sperling wants assurances that Wolfe and Archie are anti-Communist, noting that his daughter Gwen thinks Communism "intellectually contemptible and morally unsound," Wolfe responds, "We agree with your daughter"; Archie offers a saltier opinion: "a Commie is a louse," and later, "I wouldn't put anything beneath a Commie."[2] Wolfe gets in another jab too, telling the closet Communist he has exposed at the end of the book who is about to be identified by his comrades as a man wanted for murder, "You're done, . . . with your comrades spitting you out as only they can spit" (p. 241).

Politics enters the middle novels in another way—political corruption by organized crime. This is the period of the Zeck novels, and Zeck is the master corrupter. In describing Zeck's activities to the Sperling family, Wolfe includes, along with larceny, narcotics traffic, and blackmail, "political malfeasance" (p. 57). Someone "not far from the top of the New York Police Department" is in Zeck's pocket, for example, and Wolfe asserts that there are only ten people in New York of whom he could confidently say they have no connection with Zeck (pp. 59 and 67). In *In The Best Families* even Cramer tells Archie, "He is out of anybody's reach. It's a goddam crime for an officer of the law to have to say a thing like that, even privately, but it's true."[3]

Politics—not international espionage alone, but also the day-to-day functioning of the political and legal system—is seen as riddled with naivete, immaturity, misguided idealism, and downright dirty corruption. Politics has in effect taken over from the family as the arena in which Wolfe's cases are worked out; consequently it, like the family in the earlier novels, becomes tainted. Evil forces are at work there; it is dangerous. Where in the early novels man is a social animal, he is here a political one, and the switch does him little credit. Of course not all the middle novels are as explicitly political as the ones just alluded to. *Too*

Many Women, And Be A Villain, and *Before Midnight* focus on
problems of love, lust, and greed and the tensions they produce.
Yet the presence of a new element in the series is undeniable.
Its greatest impact can be seen in the new interest in unmasking.
All the political novels require anonymous or unseen persons to
be revealed—spies in *Over My Dead Body,* the faceless Zeck in
In the Best Families, the faceless Communist William Reynolds
in *The Second Confession.* Detecting always requires the unmasking of the murderer, but in the middle novels Wolfe and
Archie uncover more than murder. They reveal the inadequacy
of human attempts at self-government, just as they earlier revealed the agonies produced by our fumbling attempts to love.

The middle novels focus on the mortal battle Wolfe and Archie
wage with Arnold Zeck. It represents their greatest challenge as
a team and as individuals, their rite of passage. Up until the Zeck
trilogy, Wolfe and Archie bait each other, their relationship an
amalgam of pride and idiosyncrasy. In the first novels they
threaten continually, though comically, to break up, a response
perhaps to all the family tensions they encounter. In the middle
novels, however, the threat looms from without, not within, and
in response to that pressure Archie and Wolfe close ranks. It is
true that as part of their defense they are temporarily driven apart,
but they come together again at the end. The battle with Zeck
cements their relationship, validates their skill at detecting, and
reinforces, by its very abandonment of them, the conventions of
behavior that give the Wolfe novels their flavor.

Whenever Wolfe and Archie face a supreme challenge, they
separate. Both in the Zeck trilogy and in *A Family Affair* they
are separated—once physically, once by their information about
a murderer. But these separations ultimately turn out to be unifying experiences. After the shock of Wolfe's disappearance has
worn off, Archie remarks, "The hell of it wasn't how I felt, but
that I didn't know how to feel. If I had actually seen the last of
Nero Wolfe, it was a damn sad day for me, there were no two
ways about that, and if I got a lump in my throat and somebody
walked in I would just as soon show him the lump as not" (p.
97). And speaking of Wolfe to Zeck he observes, "I know he had
his faults—God knows how I stood them as long as I did—but

he taught me a lot, and wherever he is he's my favorite fatty" (p. 188). To Rackham he takes the separation more seriously: "It was Zeck and you, between you, that broke up our happy home on Thirty-fifth Street, and you can have three guesses how I feel about it" (p. 167). None of these is an unqualified expression of regard for Wolfe, and the latter two remarks are pitched at particular audiences for particular reasons, but expressions of mutual regard between Wolfe and Archie are rare and none are as explicit as these. Zeck offers an excuse for Archie to say what has always been clear but unspoken in the series: his regard for Wolfe is deep and personal. When Wolfe unmasks in Archie's office, even though their first act is to quibble over whether Archie had recognized him all along, the novel quickly focuses on the dictionary on Archie's desk. Wolfe says, "I see you have my dictionary here." Archie counters, "It's the one from my room which you gave me for Christmas nineteen thirty-nine" (p. 144). The gift, given and received, calls attention to the relationship that has been renewed with Wolfe's reappearance, and it looks forward to the climax of the scene: "I got up and went halfway. He got up and came halfway. As we shook, our eyes met . . ." (p. 144). The scene is comic because of Wolfe's appearance, but it is comic in the deeper sense too, celebrating union, renewal, rebirth.

Wolfe, naturally taciturn in his expressions of regard, keeps his response to their reunion low-keyed. Throughout the series his expressions of regard have been associated mainly with Archie's job performance. Everyone knows that "satisfactory" is his greatest plaudit, and certainly Archie earns it often. Here, though, Wolfe becomes a little more loquacious. "I had gone as far as I could without you," he tells Archie during their first long conversation at Lily Rowan's, and concludes, "It's vastly better this way" (pp. 149 and 150). When he departed his house in the early hours Easter morning headed for the Gulf and a month of suffering, he left notes for Theodore, Fritz, and Archie. Theodore's was signed with "My regards," Fritz's with "My best regards," and Archie's with "My very best regards and wishes" (p. 61). It took a submachine-gun attack on the orchids and a bomb threat in the house to do it, but the result is clear. By the time of *In the Best Families*, the Wolfe-Archie team has come of age.

They have matured not only as friends but as detectives as well, for in defeating Zeck, Wolfe and Archie defeat the ultimate opponent. No less a man than Inspector Cramer mournfully tells Archie that Zeck is out of reach, and Zeck himself emphasizes his stature as a challenger to Wolfe and Archie in his telephone calls by constantly reminding them, despite his admiration for Wolfe, that he has the best mind, the grandest network, the greatest influence. Defeating him then demonstrates that Wolfe and Archie truly are the best detectives anywhere. The scene that cements Wolfe and Archie as a pair also fixes them at the top of the professional heap.

Rex Stout took pains to emphasize the stakes in the race after Zeck. He does this in part by stretching the story over three novels, the only time he created a series within his series. Further, while detectives in fiction conventionally regard whatever case they are working on as the hardest of their career, and while Archie is no exception to this general rule, Stout goes to great lengths in the Zeck trilogy to emphasize both Wolfe's and Archie's mortal danger. Some examples of this are obvious—the orchid massacre, for example, or the booby-trapped sausage box, or Wolfe's enforced exile. Everyone knows that Wolfe never leaves his house on business; everyone also knows that in fact he leaves rather often—in *The Red Box*, *Too Many Cooks*, and *Some Buried Caesar*, to name three quick examples. Despite the exceptions, though, his rule is so notorious that such a complete flouting of it as occurs in the Zeck battle clearly reflects dire exigency. But there are also more subtle ways of emphasizing the danger Zeck poses. One is Wolfe's own respect for him. When he first hears of Zeck's blackmailing scheme in *And Be A Villain*, Wolfe marvels at its ingenuity. Confronted at the end of the book by the possibility that he may have to fight Zeck one day, Wolfe hopes he will not be pushed to that extreme. Describing Zeck to the Sperling family, Wolfe credits him with "unexcelled talent, a remorseless purpose, and a will that cannot be deflected" (p. 57). And he goes ahead later in the novel to describe Zeck as "the only man on earth I'm afraid of" (p. 142). Wolfe's repeated vows that if pressed to fight Zeck he will leave home, find a hideout known only to a few, and wage mortal battle from there increase this sense of Zeck's invulnerability, thereby adding to the stature Wolfe and Archie attain by defeating him. As Wolfe observes when he instructs Archie to call Fritz from Zeck's office to order dinner, "A man has a right to have his satisfactions match his pains" (p. 233). Similarly, his stature must match his accomplishments. By defeating Zeck, Wolfe and Archie earn the stature to which they lay claim.

The battle with Zeck then has both a personal and a vocational importance for the leading characters of the Wolfe series. It has moreover another crucial consequence, this one not on the level of character but on the larger level of the development of the series as a whole: through the very shocks and blows the battle with Zeck delivers to the world of the series, the victory over him becomes a reaffirmation of that world. The middle novels set the world of the series on its ear and then return its equilibrium, enforcing with that return the fixity of their fictive universe.

The keynote of the battle with Zeck is disorder. The orchids are decimated; the Wolfe household lives under siege. Wolfe admits an equal, leaves home, loses vast amounts of weight, grows a beard, consorts with a woman, even operates an illegal project on the west coast, that most un-Wolfeian of places. In short, everything is topsy-turvy. The world of the Wolfe novels, normally a meticulously, if eccentrically, ordered one, surrenders to disorder, even to the point of reversing its own values. This reversal represented Stout's chance to end the series, a la Holmes at the Reichenbach Falls. Zeck, by gaining temporary ascendancy over Wolfe, calls all into doubt. Perhaps, he seems to say, the center cannot hold after all. If it cannot, then Wolfe must be banished, Archie isolated, and a new series begun—the Archie Goodwin novels, perhaps?

The Zeck battle raises the alternative possibility that the series, if not ending, would change character. Wolfe has reached a normal weight and is mobile and active. Why not keep him this way and open up new possibilities for the novels? Even Archie urges him to stay in shape. In this precarious situation, the series moves decisively back into order. It reaffirms the values, the habits, the quirks it had been building since 1934. Chapter 22 of *In the Best Families* is unequivocal. Seventy-two hours after the death of Zeck, Wolfe has shaved, washed the hair oil off of his head, gained ten pounds, and given all the orchids a thorough inspection. The crowning—and comic—emblem of this return to order occurs when Annabel Frey, Mrs. Rackham's daughter-in-law, calls and asks Wolfe to come to Birchvale. "I'm sorry Mrs. Frey, but it's out of the question," Wolfe replies. "I transact business only in my office. I never leave it" (p. 235). This wild disregard for the events of the past five months constitutes Wolfe's final comment on the subject. With this reaffirmation of order the Wolfe-Archie relationship is newly cemented, their professional status reaffirmed, and the world they live in given a new legitimacy.

The middle novels of the Wolfe series unquestionably depart from the early novels by switching from the family to politics as a focus of interest. Yet the battle with Zeck also reaffirms the basic premises of the series. These novels, for example, continue the interest in the family. *Over My Dead Body* introduces a new element into the house on Thirty-fifth Street—a daughter. *Too Many Women* offers a complex interaction between Cecily Pine, her brilliant but warped brother Kerr Naylor, and her husband, Kerr Naylor's boss. Both Cecily Pine and Kerr Naylor admit only one weak spot—each other. This is especially striking in Cecily Pine, whom one would expect to side with her husband. The novel mixes family loyalty with lust and the hunger for power in this twisted triangle. *And Be A Villain* tells of two sisters-in-law, girlhood friends and now close business associates, their relationship queered by the fact that the person who joins them in a family bond—Deborah Koppel's brother and Madeline Fraser's husband—died the victim of arsenic poisoning. *The Second Confession* begins with the sort of family tension that characterized the early novels—a daughter whose choice of a partner has upset her family who, in turn, have come to Wolfe for help. *In the Best Families* plays heavily on this theme. Its title, one of many in the Wolfe series that reflect Stout's interest in family matters, applies both to the Rackhams and to Wolfe's family, where a mock divorce occurs.

Throughout the Wolfe series up until this point, the family has been a source both of strength and turmoil. The secure family environment has been Wolfe's despite its comic tensions. The other families, by contrast, have been the staging ground for all the violence that clouds the novels. The middle novels continue this pattern until the Zeck trilogy when the series' ideal family is shattered by the anti-family of Zeck's network of criminals. The group that has always stayed together, its bond the anti-type in its firmness of the shifty, slippery bonds that fail to hold together the families in the other books, also comes apart. The fear which lurks behind the series is realized: chaos reigns.

By the end of the Zeck trilogy, though, the integrity of Wolfe's family has been reasserted along with everything else. Archie is saying more than he realizes when he sarcastically reports that "Fritz might have been a mother whose lost little boy has been brought home after wandering in the desert for days" the way he treats Wolfe on his return (p. 233). This family reunion at the end of the trilogy is an emblem of the order, reaffirmation, and security with which the middle novels end.

5

Crack-Up:
The Late Novels

*The Final Deduction, Gambit,
A Right to Die, The Doorbell Rang,
Death of a Doxy, Please Pass the
Guilt, A Family Affair*

The Final Deduction (1961)

The Final Deduction begins with an expression of deep family concern over a kidnapping; it ends with Wolfe identifying not a kidnapper but a murderer, and the family concern with which the book opened turns out to be nothing more than a mask for greed, then lust, then, ultimately, violence.

At the opening of the novel Althea Vail, a wealthy middle-aged woman, calls upon Wolfe. Her young husband Jimmy, whom she married off the stage, has been kidnapped and is being held for $500,000 ransom. Wolfe is not to chase the kidnappers; he is merely to do everything possible to ensure Jimmy Vail's safe return. Accepting the job, he immediately places an advertisement in the newpaper informing the kidnapper of what he has undertaken to do. If Jimmy Vail is not returned unharmed after the ransom has been paid, Wolfe threatens, he will bring the kidnapper to justice no matter how long it takes or what it costs.

Only one detail about the kidnapping disturbs Wolfe: the kidnapper calls himself "Mr. Knapp." Would a serious kidnapper be in a state of mind for such drollery? His suspicions piqued, Wolfe asks to see Mrs. Vail's secretary, Dinah Utley. Under the pretext of taking her fingerprints, Archie verifies the fact that the last two fingers of her left hand are swollen and sore. The typed ransom note from Mr. Knapp is decidedly lighter on the keys those fingers would reach. This is too much coincidence for Wolfe: Dinah Utley is involved.

The next two events happen in rapid succession: Jimmy Vail is released unharmed, and Dinah Utley is found murdered on a back road in Westchester county. Vail had promised his kidnappers to say and do nothing for forty-eight hours as a condition of his release, so Wolfe continues on retainer to justify not turning the matter over to the police.

The plot remains on hold until Jimmy Vail is found dead in the library of the Vail town home the next day. The library is full of statues, reproductions of famous ones, and Vail has been crushed by Benjamin Franklin, who fell off his pedestal, onto Vail's chest. The police want to treat the matter as an accident, but Wolfe insists it was murder. Ordinarily no one would care about Wolfe's charge, nor would he have bothered to make his suspicions public since he has finished his work for Mrs. Vail, but Noel Vail, her dippy son, offers a tempting scheme which keeps Wolfe involved. Mrs. Vail has promised Noel that if he can find the $500,000 ransom paid to Mr. Knapp he can keep it. Noel in turn promises Wolfe one fifth of the money for his help. The odds are against them, but if Wolfe succeeds he will be able to read, cultivate orchids, and gourmandize until winter without taking on a new case, so he accepts.

Archie finds the ransom money in the bottom of a trunk on the Vail country estate, but this fact is less important than the larger fact that in order to find the money Wolfe figures out who killed Dinah Utley, who killed Jimmy Vail, and why. It is one of his most spectacular conclusions; he does it all by deduction with barely any help from the facts or from physical evidence, and the results are as shocking as they are strange. Wolfe was right after all to doubt a kidnapper who calls himself "Mr. Knapp."

Gambit (1962)

Gambit begins in the same way as *The Final Deduction*: a woman pleads for Wolfe's help and gets it when she urges that only a genius could do the impossible and solve her problem. Trapped by his vanity, Wolfe accepts another outlandishly difficult case. This time, though, his client is a rich young woman—Sally Blount—rather than a rich middle-aged one, and the problem centers not on a husband but a father—Matthew Blount, a prominent business man in jail charged with murder.

Blount belongs to a chess club—The Gambit Club—where he arranged an exhibition match between twelve club members on the one hand and a brilliant but erratic man—Paul Jerrin— on the other. Jerrin was to play the twelve games simultaneously. In fact, however, he fell ill during the match and was rushed to the hospital where he died, a victim of arsenic poisoning.

Blount's case appears hopeless. He had motive—he had only recently thrown Jerrin out of his house and told him to stay away from Sally. He had means—it was Blount who brought Jerrin a pot of hot chocolate just before Jerrin fell ill. And he had attracted suspicion—as soon as Jerrin fell ill, Blount took the chocolate pot to the kitchen and washed it out, destroying the evidence before putting fresh chocolate in.

Sally Blount brings her father's case to Wolfe because she believes that the man in charge of his defense—an attorney named Daniel Kalmus—loves her mother, Blount's wife. Her forthright statement of this suspicion has made her home too uncomfortable for her, since everyone, Kalmus especially, disapproves of her decision to see Wolfe. So Sally Blount moves to Wolfe's house for the duration of the case.

The only others with the means to kill Jerrin were the cook and the steward at the club and the four messengers who brought Jerrin the moves of his opponents in another room. None of these however can be shown to have any connection at all with Jerrin, let alone a convincing motive to kill him. This seemingly negative fact offers Wolfe his first clue. The real victim was not Jerrin but Blount; Jerrin was merely a pawn sacrificed to attain a larger goal—Blount's conviction. The murder was itself a gambit.

Blount's wife is one of the witch-women in the Wolfe novels, like Dina Laszio in *Too Many Cooks*, who draw men incessantly but effortlessly. Mrs. Blount, though, is an innocent witch, as unconscious of her power as she is innocent of using it. Lon Cohen feels it. Archie feels it. Even Cramer and Wolfe acknowledge it. Who from among Blount's acquaintance desired his wife desperately enough to kill for her? Sally Blount believes it is Kalmus, who has been resisting Wolfe and Archie all along. But he is found dead—strangled—in his apartment by Archie and Sally who are on a fishing expedition there. This event shocks everyone, but it is not nearly as startling as Blount's subsequent admission to Archie the next day that he had put something in Jerrin's drink that night. It hadn't been arsenic though. It was merely a solution recommended by his physician, Dr. Victor Avery, also a club member, to befuddle Jerrin without harming him. Someone had used Jerrin's illness to create an opportunity to give him the arsenic.

As soon as they hear Blount's story, Wolfe and Archie know who murdered Jerrin and Kalmus. They also know they haven't a chance of proving the Jerrin murder and only a ghost of one to prove Kalmus's. So Wolfe constructs one of his fanciest charades. The results satisfy everyone—except Inspector Cramer.

A Right to Die (1964)

A Right to Die connects in several important ways with *Too Many Cooks*. The novel opens with a black man named Whipple calling upon Wolfe. In one of the most memorable scenes from the series, Whipple quotes verbatim that speech of Wolfe's given late one night at Kanawha Spa as Wolfe tried to find the murderer of Philip Laszio. At the time Wolfe had been arguing to a group of black waiters that to shield a member of their race from the charge of murdering a white man would perpetuate rather than alleviate the wrongs of racial prejudice. It had been Paul Whipple, college student and budding anthropologist, who bought Wolfe's argu-

ment and supplied information that allowed Wolfe to name the
murderer.

Whipple, now an assistant professor of anthropology at Columbia, has come to claim the favor Wolfe owes him in return.
His son, Dunbar Whipple, plans to marry a young, beautiful,
wealthy woman—Susan Brooke, a Radcliffe graduate who vol-
unteers her time for ROCC—the Rights of Citizens Committee.
There is only one problem: she is white. Whipple, convinced
that there must be something wrong with a woman in her position
who would marry a black man, opposes such a match. He wants
Wolfe to find out what her fault is—whatever it might be—so
that Dunbar can be prevented from taking such a rash step.

The task is absurd—especially for Wolfe, who suggests that
there is probably nothing wrong with Miss Brooke beyond, "the
innate and universal flaws of her sex." Yet he had undertaken a
similar commission before for James Sperling in *The Second
Confession*, and this time he has the opportunity to discharge an
obligation. He accepts the case.

Archie investigates, both in New York and in Susan Brooke's
home town of Racine, Wisconsin, but the most startling fact he
can uncover is that a college friend of hers, one Richard Ault,
committed suicide on the front porch of her family home when
she refused to continue to see him. Susan had been cleared of
any wrongdoing at the time, and she has stayed clean.

The case appears to be a washout until Susan Brooke is brutally murdered, beaten to death with a nightstick. When the police arrive Dunbar Whipple is in the room with her body. He
had discovered it, for he had arranged to meet Susan that night
in the apartment where he found her. The police arrest him for
murder, Whipple senior is back at Wolfe's office, and Wolfe is
back on the case.

There are two groups of suspects in this case—Susan Brooke's
family, all of whom disapproved of her association with Whipple,
and her colleagues at ROCC, including Whipple, Thomas Henchey, Harold Oster, Adam Ewing, Cass Faison, Rae Kallman,
Beth Tiger, and Maud Jordan—a white spinster who donates
both her time and money to the committee.

The first apparent breakthrough occurs when Wolfe and Archie learn that Dolly Brooke, Susan's sister-in-law, had lied to

them about her movements on the night of the murder. She claims to have been at home the entire evening; in fact however she was at the apartment where Susan Brooke's body was found. She had knocked and received no answer. As she left she saw Dunbar Whipple arriving. Her admission, coerced in a typically Wolfeian way, clears Dunbar Whipple, but it does not supply a murderer to replace him, unless it is Dolly Brooke herself.

Archie buys that theory until Peter Vaughn, the erstwhile suitor of Susan Brooke whom her family had been backing, is found murdered in his car. Dolly Brooke's airtight alibi for that evening eliminates her as a suspect and, as Archie complains to Wolfe, "There isn't one single solitary sensible thing that you can do or I can do or Saul and Fred and Orrie can do." This situation remains at a frustrating standstill until Wolfe reflects, in desperation, on a diphthong. That reflection leads to a phone call, the phone call to a trip to Indiana for Archie, and the trip to Indiana to a murderer in New York. It turns out that the suicide of Richard Ault was not totally irrelevant after all, and it further turns out that in a novel concerned with people's civil rights there is one person obsessed by another right—the right to die.

The Doorbell Rang (1965)

In *The Doorbell Rang* Nero Wolfe takes on one of his toughest opponents ever—the FBI. In a novel that offers a sixties parallel to the great battle against Zeck of the forties, Wolfe and Archie undertake the impossible and make it possible, a feat that brings a broad smile even to the face of Inspector Cramer.

The novel begins with Rachel Bruner, the tremendously wealthy widow of real estate magnate Lloyd Bruner, calling on Wolfe. She had read an exposé of the FBI—*The FBI Nobody Knows*—and been so impressed that she had sent ten thousand copies of it to influential people throughout the country. The FBI has retaliated by tapping her telephone, bugging her office, and blatantly following her and her associates around. Her job for Wolfe is to make them stop; her offer is a $100,000 retainer, all expenses paid, and a fee to be determined by him. Archie prudently opposes the job, but Wolfe cannot turn it down for the same reason he could not resist a showdown with Zeck: his pride will not permit him to refuse a job merely because he fears the opponent. He is committed.

Using leads supplied by Lon Cohen, Archie tries to catch on to illegal operations the FBI has pulled recently in New York, but he gets nowhere until an anonymous caller invites him to a meeting in a dingy hotel. Archie arrives to find Inspector Cramer and a carton of milk, Cramer's gift, waiting for him. Cramer has heard about Wolfe's job. The FBI wants the police commissioner to revoke Wolfe's and Archie's detective licenses, and before he recommends for or against such a move, Cramer wants to know what is going on. In appreciation for the carton of milk, Archie tells him. Cramer reciprocates with information about an unsolved murder in which the FBI is entangled. Morris Althaus, a free-lance writer, had been doing an investigative piece on the FBI for *Tick-Tock* magazine when he was found shot to death in his apartment. The material he had collected was gone, the bullet had been dug out of the wall, and a witness saw three FBI men leaving the building the evening of the murder. The FBI has refused to cooperate with Cramer who, infuriated, believes they shot Althaus.

Archie and Wolfe begin investigating the Althaus murder. If the FBI killed Althaus, they must be able to prove it so they can use that fact for leverage; if they did not, Archie and Wolfe want to know who did, but they must find out without letting the FBI know. At all costs, the head of the FBI must believe, whether it is true or not, that Wolfe can prove his men shot Althaus. The investigation turns up some interesting facts: Althaus knew Mrs. Bruner; one of his pieces on a realty scam led to the jailing of a Bruner employee; and he lives directly above Mrs. Bruner's attractive secretary, Sarah Dacos. Though he had been engaged at the time of his murder, Althaus had a reputation as a ladies' man.

Wolfe finally feels ready to spring his trap. He and Archie plant an article in the newspaper announcing that they will be out on Long Island as guests of a gourmet society on a specific night. They hire actors their size and shape who leave from the brownstone in their place, and they wait in the darkened house for the FBI to try a bag job. They do, and Wolfe has caught them red-handed. He can now satisfy Mrs. Bruner at any time, but he wishes also to satisfy Inspector Cramer, especially since Archie discovers that Althaus was not murdered by FBI agents. The result is a final confrontation between Cramer and Richard Wragg, head G-man in New York, with Wolfe in the unlikely role of mediator. He is satisfied however. With his retainer and his fee it will be months before he need even consider taking up another case.

Death of a Doxy (1966)

In *Death of a Doxy* Wolfe works for Orrie Cather rather than Orrie for him. What's more, there is no prospect of a fee until nearly the end of the novel, and then it is not Orrie who pays.

The novel begins with Archie in a murdered woman's apartment kneeling beside her corpse, cold on the floor. The woman is Isabel Kerr, a sometime chorus girl and one of Orrie's countless mistresses. The problem was that Orrie had finally decided to marry an airline stewardess named Jill Hardy, but when he broke the news to Isabel Kerr she threatened to ruin the marriage, claiming to be pregnant with Orrie's child. To prove her determination to go to court she was holding hostage Orrie's private detective's license and other things she had taken from him one night. Orrie's solution is devious, but it promises to work. Giving Archie his key to Isabel's apartment, he asks him to go there on Saturday afternoon while she is at her weekly date with her sister Stella and to swipe all Orrie's belongings. When he arrives at the apartment, all Archie finds is Isabel's corpse. He doesn't stay.

When the police learn about Orrie's problem with Kerr from her diary, they jail Orrie as a material witness while Cramer looks for enough evidence to charge him. Just as quickly Wolfe, more out of regard for his own name than out of affection for Orrie, undertakes to clear him. This situation is complicated by the fact that Isabel Kerr was also the mistress of Avery Ballou, an extraordinarily wealthy financier who was paying for her apartment and her living expenses in exchange for her favors. Wolfe and Archie know this because they learn it from Orrie. Isabel's sister knows it too, and it galls her deeply. As Archie learns in speaking to her and her husband, Barry Fleming, a mathematics teacher,

Stella practically raised her sister single-handedly, and she would do anything to keep Isabel's circumstances from becoming public knowledge.

Wolfe gets nowhere with his inquiries. He interviews Avery Ballou and Isabel Kerr's best friend, a nightclub singer called Julie Jaquette, and Archie talks to Ballou's wife and to the Flemings. Saul and Fred inquire into Isabel's circle from the theater. Nothing. Then Avery Ballou pays a surprise call. For the past five months he has been blackmailed by someone calling himself "Milton Thales" who demands a thousand dollars a month not to tell about Ballou's recreation. Ballou assumes the caller was Orrie, but the name Milton Thales tells Wolfe who the blackmailer really is. His job now is to prove that the blackmailer is also Isabel's murderer. If he can do it without revealing the name of her provider, Ballou will give him fifty thousand dollars.

Julie Jaquette becomes the bait as Wolfe and Archie try to lure Milton Thales into a deadly trap. Julie nearly dies, Fred does in fact get wounded, and Thales succumbs, but not in the way Wolfe had planned. At the end of the novel Orrie has been freed and has married his stewardess; Julie Jaquette is gone, leaving a void in Archie's heart; and Wolfe is at ease, his professional family once again intact.

Please Pass the Guilt (1973)

Please Pass the Guilt is one of the Wolfe novels that begins with Wolfe in need of money. In the past Wolfe has solicited clients, but here Archie does it alone without Wolfe's prior approval. It all begins when Doctor Vollmer asks a favor for a colleague who runs a crisis intervention clinic. A man who refuses to give his name has come to the clinic with the Lady Macbeth syndrome—he has blood on his hands which no one else can see and which will not go away. The director of the clinic cannot penetrate the man's defenses; will Wolfe try? Wolfe agrees, and by a simple trick he and Archie coerce the man into supplying his name. He is Kenneth Meer, an employee of Continental Air Network where a bomb had killed a vice president in his office recently.

Archie, seeing an opportunity, writes to Mrs. Peter Odell, the rich widow of the vice president killed in the blast, saying that he hates to see a case bungled and that Wolfe knows something the police do not. His letter has its desired effect, and Wolfe has a client, a $20,000 retainer, and an impossible task. Its complexity stems from the fact that Peter Odell was killed by a bomb planted in the office of another vice president—Amory Browning. Odell and Browning were the two finalists in the competition to see who would become president of CAN, so the chief question is this: was the bomb intended for Browning? for Odell? for Browning's beautiful secretary and lover Helen Lugos? for someone else?

After Wolfe has accepted her retainer, Mrs. Odell supplies some extraordinary information. Her husband had been in Browning's office to put LSD into the bourbon supply he kept there. Browning always took a drink in the late afternoon, and Odell had hoped to so bewilder him with the LSD that he would ruin his chances for the presidency of CAN. Mrs. Odell further claims that her secretary, who had procured the LSD in the first place, found out about the plan and, fearing for Browning's life, had warned him in advance of the plot. The client's conclusion: Browning planted the bomb.

But Wolfe and Archie discover that their client is lying. Convinced that Browning had somehow killed her husband, Mrs. Odell has bribed her mousy secretary to claim she had warned Browning in advance; in fact however he had been away at the time and never could have received such a warning. Wolfe and Archie are enraged, the client is mortified, and the hunt begins anew.

Further investigation reveals nothing. Finally Wolfe is prepared to declare defeat and return his retainer until Archie conceives another stratagem: Mrs. Odell offers a reward of $65,000 for information about her husband's death, the reward to be administered by Wolfe. Among all the crackpot calls is one serious one. Dennis Copes, a CAN employee, claims to have overheard Meer warning Helen Lugos to stay away from Browning's desk the day of the explosion. Copes's story is a lie, but it leads to the truth, and the truth sheds new light on the Lady Macbeth syndrome from which Meer suffers. The patient cannot minister to

himself; Wolfe must be both scourge and minister as he sorts out
the truth from among the CAN intrigues. The bomb was intended
for neither Browning nor Odell, but Wolfe earns his fee by ex-
posing both the intended victim and the mad bomber who is left
quivering alone in the front hall of the brownstone while the
homicide squad sends someone to pick him up and to defuse the
bomb he has brought with him.

A Family Affair (1975)

A Family Affair was Rex Stout's last novel, and in his own words,
"the best plot I've ever thought of."[1] Full of the autumnal qualities one might expect from such a work, it is a novel of ripe old
friendships, of hidden vulnerability, of sudden and sad endings.
In tone it is quite unlike any other Nero Wolfe novel.

The book begins with a violent ending. Pierre Ducos, Wolfe's
favorite waiter at Rusterman's, calls at the brownstone late one
winter evening. Someone is trying to kill him, but he refuses to
tell Archie anything about the affair: he must see Wolfe. Un-
willing to awaken Wolfe and too tired to work on Pierre, Archie
puts him in the guest room for the night. Moments later a bomb
explodes there, killing Pierre and destroying the room. A quick
search before he calls the police tells Archie only one thing:
Pierre was murdered by a bomb concealed in a Don Pedro cigar
tube which he had apparently found in his coat pocket and which
had exploded into his face when he unscrewed the cap to look
inside.

Enraged, Wolfe immediately begins an investigation without
a client and without a fee. Interviews with Pierre's co-workers
at Rusterman's reveal only one suggestive fact: he bet on horse
races. A conversation with his father, who speaks only French
and will discuss his son only with Wolfe, reveals another: one
of Pierre's customers had left a slip of paper with a man's name
on it on a tray a week ago, and just before he was murdered a
man—perhaps the same one, perhaps not—had given him a
hundred dollars for that slip of paper. This fact becomes even
more suggestive when it turns out that the man who had left the
slip of paper on the tray was Harvey H. Bassett, a wealthy elec-

tronics executive who had himself been murdered that week. Wolfe knows a coincidence when he sees it, and this is not one. He immediately puts Saul, Fred, and Orrie on the trails of the six men who were at dinner with Bassett the night the slip of paper was left behind. Wolfe clashes with Manhattan Homicide on nearly every case he undertakes, but in this case it is all-out war. Wolfe stands mute on the murder, publicly asserting that he hopes the police do not catch the murderer so he can have the satisfaction of doing it himself. The inevitable ensues. Lucille Ducos, Pierre's feminist daughter, is murdered outside the Ducos apartment on a Saturday morning, and the police learn that Wolfe has been investigating and holding back information. Confronted with his obvious guilt, Wolfe steadfastly refuses to talk. Archie is amazed, Cramer flabbergasted, and Saul, Fred, and Orrie quizzical, but Wolfe remains silent.

Only after they are out on bail and Wolfe still refuses to speak or act does Archie catch on. This murder is indeed a family affair. The clues, once seen, are obvious. The key fact is that Bassett was obsessed with his wife, a former showgirl with the ridiculous stage name of Doraymee. But naming the murderer is not nearly as hard as knowing what to do with him. And that in turn is not nearly as hard as living with that decision. This is the only novel in which Wolfe and Archie, after wrapping up the case, must try to go to sleep.

ANALYSIS OF THEMES

The last Wolfe novels conclude the series by drawing together its principal themes and recapitulating its motifs. This orchestration is admirable because it is technically adept; however it is more than that. It is also moving. The tone is mellow. Both Archie and Wolfe admit to a vulnerability they have concealed from the reader up until now. Friendships—both professional and personal—become more important than ever, and character moves increasingly into the foreground. In these ways the Wolfe series moves toward its conclusion with a somber wisdom which it offers as the fruit of experience.

The first sign of conclusion in the series is the merging of its two main themes: family relationships and politics. In the early Wolfe novels Rex Stout probed the institution of the family. On the one hand it was a seedbed for violence, the intimate violence that springs from sins committed within the bosom of the family—infidelity, jealousy, greed, lust—all issuing in revenge, which turns out to be killing out of distorted love. On the other hand, those early novels also portrayed the family as a model for justice and order. Wolfe and his family in the brownstone on West Thirty-fifth Street are one example; Wolfe's professional family is another. Here the family is a source of loyalty, respect, affection, repose. In the middle novels this family interest continued, but it receded into the background, giving way to an interest in politics. These novels saw the human animal not only as a domestic creature but also as a political one: the masks which the series had penetrated in the small compass of a family were worn by people struggling for control of entire nations.

In the last novels these two interests merge. The central novels of this last group—*A Right to Die*, *The Doorbell Rang*, and *A Family Affair*—all revolve around political issues—race relations, the integrity and credibility of the FBI, and Watergate. But this concern is firmly anchored in the kinds of family issues which give depth to the entire series. *A Right to Die* probes parent-child relationships at that problematic moment when a child wants to marry. *The Doorbell Rang* poses a threat to the Wolfe families—an invasion of their home and office. *A Family Affair* takes that invasion—which was invited and prepared for—and turns it on its head by offering a totally unexpected and uninvited invasion of the family. The interaction of these themes provides the main interest of the last novels.

One of the most striking attitudes to emerge from the middle Wolfe novels was Wolfe's deep distrust of political maneuvering. *Over My Dead Body* expressed his contempt for espionage, intrigue, and political violence. In fact, it attacked political idealism as empty, naive, and even potentially corrupting. *The Doorbell Rang* and *A Family Affair*, both of which focus on power-hungry figures of the American political scene, extend this harsh view to domestic politics. These novels object to misuse of power and to deception, especially to deception. In talking to Richard

Wragg, the head of the FBI in New York, Wolfe calls one of his statements "a routine lie."[2] When Cramer and Wragg start to wrangle over how to resolve the problem of explaining the Althaus murder in court without involving the FBI, Cramer maintains, "My men are not perjurers." Wolfe retorts, "save your posing for audiences that will appreciate it. This one isn't sufficiently naive" (p. 183). Indeed Wolfe's whole trap in this novel is predicated on the shocking fact that Wragg cannot trust his own men to tell the truth about whether they murdered Althaus; they have to take the murder bullet out of the wall and bring it to him to convince him it was not theirs. Similarly in *A Family Affair* the political cynicism of the Watergate era springs from Wolfe's and Archie's disgust at Presidential perfidy. Wolfe is reading Fitzgerald's translation of the *Iliad*. Archie comments, "So he sat and read about a phony horse instead of a phony statesman."[3] In *A Right to Die* deception becomes a political issue as well when the murderer turns out to be a civil rights worker who has been harboring a deep and vicious hatred of blacks all during her masquerade as a humanitarian. *A Family Affair* does also praise voting in what seems to be an expression of faith in democracy. Archie observes, "It's the only time I feel important and know I have a right to." But this brief note of idealism modulates at once to cynicism: "Sometimes the feeling lasts all the way home if somebody doesn't bump me" (p. 111).

This cynicism is not new. But in these last novels the political cynicism leaks into the theme of the family, coloring it a somber shade, upsetting the balance of colors that had reflected the series's equilibrium up until this point. In the Wolfe novels Stout offers a pessimistic view of the family and an idealistic one, sustaining a creative tension between them throughout the early and middle novels. The middle novels also introduced the political cynicism that colors them without offering a corresponding idealized view. As though that were enough to tip the scales, to upset as it were the equilibrium of these themes, the idealized view of the family loses much of its force at the end of the series. The cynicism of Wolfe's politics breeds a corresponding cynicism in his view of the family, and the series ends not with affirmation but with doubt, not with repose but with unrest.

Neither *The Final Deduction* nor *Gambit* concerns itself with politics. Both however show an interest in the family. *The Final Deduction* revolves around family violence of the kind we are accustomed to from the early novels. *Gambit* offers in a sense an antitype to that novel, for the leading character, Sally Blount, suspects such violence but does not find it. A brutal murder occurs, but its source lies outside the family. These novels signal the intention of the Wolfe series to return to the family context from which they began. As such they mark the beginning of the merging of the themes.

A Right to Die sounds again the note of political pessimism which entered the series in the middle novels. The Rights of Citizens Committee, the political action group for which Dunbar Whipple works, fights discrimination against blacks. Its very existence therefore expresses faith in the political process and in the goals of democracy. Wolfe, in a gesture that would seem to belie his own eloquent cynicism, even contributes money to the group. Yet we see it as deeply flawed. Its counsel, Harold Oster, is self-important, blustery, and ineffectual. Thomas Henchey, the executive director, places the good name of ROCC above the demands of justice: he and his colleagues are prepared to stonewall it to the police after Peter Vaughn's visit to their office appears to be part of the cause of his murder. Worst of all they harbor a viper in their bosom in the murderer, whose professed concern for social justice turns out to be merely a sham. In fact this is one of those novels where politics and the family intersect, for the murder of Susan Brooke turns out to be both political and familial—a crime against a person in retribution for a family grievance and a crime against a race. Intimate violence and politics merge in the same crime. The difference between this merger of themes and Stout's previous separation of them appears in the distance between this novel and its parallel one, *Too Many Cooks*. That novel, in which the reader first meets Paul Whipple, also told the story of a domestic crime, for Phillip Laszio died a victim of infidelity and lust. It also contained a political theme, for Wolfe believed the murderer was black and tried to squeeze his name out of the black employees of Kanawha Spa. In fact it is the speech he makes to them that night in West Virginia that Paul Whipple quotes at the beginning of *A Right to*

Die. Yet in *Too Many Cooks* the domestic and political plots move farther and farther apart as the novel progresses. The murderer was not a black after all, and so the issue of prejudice is ultimately lost in the resolution of the plot. Not so in the later book. There the plot links politics and the family from the start, and the links only become stronger as the novel develops. In the end both are flawed, as though neither could withstand the influence of the other, and only Wolfe and Archie and the Whipple family offer another, more optimistic, view.

The Doorbell Rang is the most cynical of the political Wolfe novels. Everyone in the book is cynical about the FBI—Mrs. Bruner, Wolfe and Archie, Lon Cohen and Cramer, the staff at *Tick-Tock* magazine, Althaus's parents. This cynicism hangs over the novel like a fog that obscures what are normally familiar landmarks. Archie's conversation with Fritz in which he explains the case illustrates the mood:

> I picked up the fork. "You know what the FBI is."
> "But certainly. Mr. Hoover."
> "That's what he thinks. On behalf of a client we're going to push his nose in . . . ."
> "But he—he's a great man. Yes?"
> "Sure. But I suppose you've seen pictures of him."
> "Yes."
> "What do you think of his nose?"
> "Not good. Not exactly *épaté*, but broad. Not *bien fait.*"
> "Then it should be pushed." I forked sausage. (p. 22)

Archie's pungent colloquialism and his irreverent "That's what he thinks" startle Fritz when applied to the great J. Edgar Hoover. Yet the tone of this speech suits the final gesture of the book, when Hoover calls at the brownstone only to be ignored by Wolfe: "Let him get a sore finger" (p. 186). This cynicism carries over into the office politics of CAN in *Please Pass the Guilt.* Peter J. Odell and Amory Browning were competing for the same job at CAN. The day of their interviews with the Board of Directors Odell planned to put LSD in Browning's drink. This shocking strategy is not known to many of those involved in Odell's murder, but those who do know of it seem relatively undisturbed. Even Wolfe permits himself only the mild observation that "adul-

terating a rival's whiskey" is not something he would do, but
"tastes and methods differ."[4]

This is not to say that in the late Wolfe novels there is a sudden
and inexplicable rush of cynicism that gives them a remarkably
new coloring. Wolfe and Archie have always been hard-headed
in the way that their profession demands. Nevertheless, there is
no denying the political disillusionment of *A Doorbell Rang* and
A Family Affair, just as there is no denying the dark view of
family relations presented in the Wolfe novels. But the family,
for all its violent undercurrents, has always been idealized in the
vision of the Wolfe family. In the last novel of the series, however,
that ideal collapses. The cynicism of politics merges with the
already present dark view of the family to tip and finally to topple
the scale which balanced the Wolfe family against the flawed
families encountered in the novels. The bastion of order and
justice and humanity had its comic cracks and flaws; here at the
end of the series those flaws become serious, perhaps even tragic,
and the order of Rex Stout's universe is gone.

The central event of the middle novels was the battle against
Zeck. In the course of this struggle Wolfe and Archie were forced
apart, forced out of their home, forced even to collaborate with
criminals. Yet in the end they triumph, returning home to their
habits and routines, reestablishing the fundamental patterns that
order the universe of the Wolfe novels.

The last novels pose a similar threat. Again Wolfe and Archie
are driven apart—though this time the distance cannot be measured physically—and again they recover from the attack to
emerge victorious. This time however order is not reestablished
and fundamental patterns are not resumed. The sense of evil in
the later novels is stronger than in the earlier ones, as is the sense
of loss. The difference between the middle and late novels can
be measured in the difference between *In the Best Families* and
A Family Affair. The parallel between these titles is by no means
coincidental. Both involve threats to a family—Wolfe's family.
Consequently, both call into question the ideal which the series
has held up to balance its dark undercurrents. The word "family"
in each title therefore signals the central importance of each book
to the series.

From its beginning, A *Family Affair* is more weighty and more somber than earlier Wolfe novels. When Pierre Ducos brings his trouble to Wolfe's door late one night Archie begins their conversation about the threat to Pierre's life with his usual banter. Pierre however is serious: "Death is not a joke." "Sure it is," Archie replies, equally serious: "It's life that's not a joke" (p. 2). Both Archie's comment and his tone seem extraordinary here. He is not given to philosophy; he is the master of fact, the human tape recorder. His comment comes as a surprise, and so does the world-weary tone, sounded again a few pages further on. After the explosion, after the invasion of police, after his talk with Stebbins, Archie locks the door: "There wasn't much of anything left in me" (p. 12). The last serious invasion of the brownstone had been Zeck's tear-gas sausage which could have been a bomb. This attack is more deadly, more brutal, more indirect; accordingly, Archie's response is more exhausted, disillusioned, empty.

In the orchid attack, the only person in danger had been Theodore, whom Archie dislikes anyway. Here it is Pierre who is in danger. So is Wolfe however and Archie's relief at seeing him well signals the deadly seriousness of the attack. "I hope," he recalls, "my voice didn't squeak from the pleasure of seeing him" (p. 5). Wolfe is not killed. He is however as he puts it, "in a rage and out of control" (p. 30). Thus he is present, but in absentia. "You have always trusted my judgement and followed instructions without question," he tells his family. "Now you can't" (p. 64). This is partly why he stands mute to Cramer, Parker, and even Archie when he learns the identity of the murderer. It is also the reason Archie takes matters into his own hands at the end of the book when he too knows the identity of the murderer: "As far as I'm concerned, you're out of it" (p. 132). Wolfe is not the center of control in this novel as he had been in all the others.

With his abdication, order disappears. This fact indicates the depth and seriousness of the issue at stake in this novel. It does not however identify the issue itself. For that one must return to the title: it is the family. Close attention to the language of this novel provides the evidence for this claim, for its most important word is "family." Wolfe breaks all his rules in this novel, just as he did in his battle with Zeck. Archie's explanation: it's a family affair. At Rusterman's the day after Pierre's death, Wolfe discusses business during a meal. Archie explains, "Business is never to be mentioned at the table, but since there was no client and no prospect of a fee, this was all in the family and therefore wasn't business" (p. 22). After the meal Wolfe wants to take a cab to Pierre's home—an unheard-of event. Archie comments, "It certainly was all in the family. For a client, no matter how urgent or how big a fee, it had never come to this and never would" (p. 23). When Wolfe and Archie discuss the case with Saul, Fred, and Orrie, Orrie offers to donate his time since it's all in the family. Wolfe replies, "This is my affair." Archie however corrects him: "I live here. . . . I took him up to that room. It's a family affair." It takes Fred to clarify the issue: "I've got two families. I don't live here like Archie, but I like to think this is my *professional* family" (p. 67). This conversation, more than any other, shows the extent of the threat. It strikes at both of Wolfe's families, at his personal and professional lives. The two become one in this novel, as Archie has explained, because of the gravity of this threat to Wolfe's order. At the end of the meeting just described, Archie can usher out "the members of the family," but he cannot usher out the gravity of his problem.

The title of this novel rings with irony. In a direct and obvious way, this investigation is all in the family. Wolfe is solving this murder for his own satisfaction, not for a client or a fee. The same holds true for Archie. The murder of a man in Wolfe's house was an offense against the family, and the family undertakes to answer that offense not only to satisfy the law but to satisfy themselves. But the phrase "all in the family" has a more sinister implication. If this case is truly *all* in the family, the criminal belongs to the family too. The case is all in the family in the sense that the offense was committed against the family by one of its own members, and that the action of the novel will be an exposure of this person. In this way the phrase becomes both an expression of solidarity and an acknowledgment of betrayal. Wolfe must sense this when he tries to insist that the case is not a family affair but his affair, just as the others must sense it when they refuse to surrender the phrase. And it is all of this that gives such weight to Archie's last use of this powerful, ambiguous phrase: "It was like getting the idea that a member of your family had committed three murders. A family affair. Would you have known?" (p. 148).

It is the gravity of this plot that accounts for the loss of equilibrium at the end of the Wolfe novels. Wolfe and Archie have grown accustomed to discovering horrible truths about others but not about "a guy we have worked and played pinochle with," as Archie puts it (p. 135). That is why in the past to name a murderer meant essentially to resolve a case. Here the identification of the killer, far from resolving the case, turns it on its head. When Cramer comes to complain about Archie's way of handling the murderer, Wolfe assures him, "I'm at peace." But Archie, who has performed some anguishing tasks that day, can only hope "that by bedtime I would be at peace too" (p. 146). Like most of his conversations with Wolfe, this one enrages Cramer. He leaves on this tart note: "I'm going home and try to get some sleep. You probably have never had to try to get some sleep. You probably never will." Wolfe seems by his silence to assent, but after Cramer leaves he asks Archie to bring Fritz and some brandy. "We'll try to get some sleep" (pp. 151–52).

As the Wolfe series develops and matures, its interest in character comes to dominate more and more over its interest in plot. This increased emphasis on character—subtle but marked—grows out of Rex Stout's treatment of his themes, which accounts for its seeming naturalness and inevitability. For, as the series gradually darkens to its conclusion, as the ideal of the family weakens and finally topples, the novels face the problem of how characters which up until now have been remarkable for their faith in order and their reliance on routine will react to their brave new world.

This interest in character differs from the heavy psychological emphasis of the early novels. There, psychology served as a tool of detection as much as anything. It was his understanding of the workings of personality that enabled Wolfe to understand Paul Chapin and others. The interest in psychology was also inevitable, given those early novels' concern with family dynamics. Novels that probe human development and the ways it can become skewed must be psychological. But in these last novels one sees not so much psychology as ethics. The new emphasis on character here raises not only the question of why people behave

as they do but also of how to evaluate that behavior and how to
trace its roots in character. These last novels do not rush to judgment, but they make ethical judgments more willingly than the
earlier ones had. *Death of a Doxy* offers a good example. One
cannot help noticing its relative lack of interest in plot for its own
sake. Only one murder occurs, Archie himself discovers the body,
the circle of suspects is small, and there are no particularly odd
or perplexing incidents to contend with. The case is difficult, but
its difficulty springs from the reticence of one of those involved
rather than from the circumstances themselves. In fact Wolfe
names the murderer only slightly past the halfway mark of the
novel. This is rare in crime fiction and in Rex Stout in particular.
Death of a Doxy takes such little interest in plot because it
emphasizes character. It is particularly interested in the relationship between Archie and Orrie Cather. Archie believes Orrie
wants his job, and Archie trusts Orrie only because Wolfe does.
Moreover Archie believes that Orrie might be a murderer when
he first meets with him after finding the body of Isabel Kerr.
These three attitudes get juggled in the novel. They even become
the subject of discussion when Saul, Fred, and Archie meet with
Wolfe to decide whether or not Orrie is innocent—a meeting
with an eerie resemblance to the "family" meetings of *A Family
Affair* where Wolfe again takes the rare step of asking the help's
opinion.

  The novel does more than probe Archie and Orrie's relationship; it also judges Orrie. Explaining the background of the case
to Wolfe, Archie says of Orrie, "While he is no Saul Panzer, for
years he has come in very handy for you—okay, for us. He has
done a lot of pretty good chores and has never skunked as far as
we know."[5] At the same time, though, he says of his errand,
"Such a chore for Saul or Fred, of course, but while I have nothing against Orrie, I wouldn't borrow his socks" (p. 18). When
Fritz hears Orrie's name connected with the case he slips out
with, "I'm glad it's Orrie instead of Saul or Fred" (p. 33). Even
Wolfe makes a judgment: "I have no affection for him; he has
frequently vexed me" (p. 24). In fact it is in the course of this
remark that Wolfe dissects and diagnoses Orrie's character: "he
has not the dignity of a man who has found his place and occupies
it, as you have Fred; nor the integrity of one who knows his

superiority but restricts it to areas that are acceptable to him, as you have, Saul." With neither dignity nor integrity, Orrie, though he is aquitted in the novel, stands convicted in the court of character.

A Family Affair has a similar interest in both character and ethics. First Wolfe and then Archie and the others realize who murdered Harvey Basset, Pierre Ducos, and his daughter because of what they know of the killer's character. The novel does not dwell on this fact however. Unlike the early novels it meditates on the ethics of handling the murderer rather than his psychology. As the murderer is told: "You've bought it, and we're going to deliver it" (p. 139). Betrayal of trust is his crime against the family, and it is the retribution, not the fine points of how the murderer was identified, that dominate the novel's conclusion.

A Right to Die offers yet another example of the concern with character and ethics at the end of the Wolfe series. Its title alone raises this issue with its suggestion of rights. The title is ironic of course. The murderer, who uses the phrase, actually means not that Susan Brooke had a right to die but that the murderer had a right to kill her, a right that the novel emphatically denies. The title is appropriate in a novel filled with talk of rights—civil rights, legal rights, moral rights. Curiously the murderer's other obsession is with character, for at the end of the novel the discussion between Wolfe and the murderer focuses on precisely why Susan Brooke had to die. Her insane monologue centers on why the murderer had to kill her almost as much as on why the victim had to die.

Thus the Wolfe novels end in a way that seems most appropriate for a series so long in the developing and so broad in its concerns. Like an individual grown old, mellow, and wise, the series concludes with the highest form of human knowledge, ethics. It moves from psychology through politics to ethics, from a study of the individual through the study of the group to an evaluation of broadly human concerns.

We want to believe the fond dream that experience brings wisdom, and in the Wolfe series it does. But wisdom does not necessarily bring happiness. At the end of the series Wolfe and Archie, the exemplars of and fighters for order, confront disorder in their most intimate relationship—their family. Their trust had been misplaced, their confidence abused, their character judgment invalidated. This is not perhaps tragic wisdom, but it is related to it, for within it also lies an affirmation. The breaking of the family circle leads ultimately to a tightening of what is left of it, to the forming of a new, if smaller, circle. At the end of the series the universe of the novels is darker, but its intimacy remains, and we sense that its order will be reestablished. The sad wisdom of experience closes the series. As an end note it is not as optimistic as some readers might wish, but it is something more important—it is human. The series tells of a growth in wisdom which accompanies a growth in sadness. The two coexist, and a new equilibrium lies within reach.

6

Nero Wolfe:
The Incurable Romantic

> I am an incurable romantic.
>> *Too Many Cooks*
>
> I am a genius.
>> *Fer-de-Lance*
>
> All genius is distorted, even my own.
>> *The League of Frightened Men*

Nero Wolfe himself supplied the key to his own character and his role in the Rex Stout novels when he made this observation to Nancy Osgood in *Some Buried Caesar*:

> I am a hired instrument of vengeance. . . .Nowadays an Erinys wears a coat and trousers and drinks beer and works for pay, but the function is unaltered and should still be performed, if at all, mercilessly. (p. 138)

It is impossible—or at least pointless—to consider Wolfe's character in the abstract. He is above all else a detective, one who pursues violators of the social order. For all his idiosyncracies, his brilliance, his clear-mindedness, we would not be interested in him outside of the context of crime: all of his other qualities serve this central mission in one way or another. The pursuit of crime constitutes the unifying purpose of Wolfe's character. Anyone who has read the Wolfe novels knows the basic biographical facts about Wolfe. He is of Montenegrin descent and spent at least part of his youth engaged in political intrigue on behalf of that country. During the Wolfe novels however he is an American citizen, living and working in New York, where he owns a three-story brownstone on West Thirty-fifth Street which he leaves as rarely as possible. His life is arranged around a rigid schedule: he breakfasts at eight o'clock in his bedroom; from nine to eleven he cultivates orchids in the greenhouse on his roof; from eleven until one-fifteen he is available in his office; lunch is at one-fifteen. Wolfe is available again after lunch until four o'clock, when he spends another two hours with the orchids, after which he is available until dinner at seven-thirty. Wolfe, who loves good food, is enormously fat, weighing perhaps two hundred eighty pounds. He is a voracious reader, an indefatigable talker, and a sublime intellect. However these, as Wolfe would say, are merely facts, not phenomena. For the important truths about his character one must probe deeper.

Wolfe is a romantic. He asserts this fact repeatedly throughout the early novels. "I suffer from a romantic conscience," he observes in *Fer-de-Lance* (p. 207); and again, "I have the romantic temperament" (p. 288). In *Too Many Cooks* he reminds Louis Servan that while he does usually insist on large fees, "I am also an incurable romantic" (p. 119), and in *Some Buried Caesar* his allowing the killer to commit suicide rather than endure prison is, in Archie's words, "one of his romantic impulses" (p. 291). In a similar situation at the end of *Over My Dead Body* Wolfe himself muses, "I wish I could cure myself of those idiotic romantic gestures" (p. 293).

In the Wolfe novels "romantic" refers to one who holds to ideal notions of human organization, conduct, worth. A romantic is an optimist, an idealist, a believer in order, dignity, truth. His romanticism can express itself in insignificant, comic moments or in the grandest, most weighty contexts. Always, though, it asserts an ideal conception of things in the face of grim reality. Here is a relatively slight example of Wolfe's romanticism. In *Too Many Cooks* when a delegation from the fifteen masters headed by his host, Louis Servan, offers him eleven thousand francs to clear Berin, Wolfe explodes:

> Confound it! . . . Apparently, sir, Marko has informed you of my
> rapacity. He was correct; I need lots of money and ordinarily my
> clients get soaked. But he could have told you I am also an in-

curable romantic. To me the relationship of host and guest is sacred. The guest is a jewel resting on the cushion of hospitality. The host is king, in his parlor and in his kitchen, and should not condescend to a lesser rôle.[1]

Of course he will take the case. He will not however take the eleven thousand francs. Wolfe's ideal conception of the relationship between host and guest prevails over his very real, but very mundane, need for money.

This incident is comic, despite its serious undertones. For one thing, Wolfe's rhetoric here is slightly overblown. As Vukcic replies, "Damn all the words." Also we know that Wolfe desperately wants Berin's recipe for *saucisse minuit*, and that to clear him will be his best means of extracting that closely held secret. But this scene merely prepares us for a much more serious and significant companion scene later in the same novel. Again Wolfe asserts the claims of the ideal over the way of the world, but this time it is justice at stake. Wolfe is explaining to a roomful of black waiters from Kanawha Spa why they should not shield a known murderer simply because he is black:

> The ideal human agreement is one in which distinctions of race and color and religion are totally disregarded; anyone helping to preserve those distinctions is postponing that ideal; and you are certainly helping to preserve them. (p. 173)

Here the word "ideal" characterizes Wolfe's vision. The underlying optimism of the passage appears in the phrase "postponing that ideal," which assumes that the ideal human agreement will one day prevail—the only question is when. This is the serious side of romanticism in the Wolfe novels, the one that proposes an alternative to the tawdry world of crime and criminals which surrounds and sometimes invades Wolfe's brownstone.

Wolfe's romanticism extends beyond the idea that there is such a thing as an ideal human agreement. In that same conversation with the Kanawha Spa staff he explains that he would never use physical violence to extract the murderer's name: "I wouldn't use physical violence even if I could, because one of my romantic ideas is that physical violence is beneath the dignity of a man, and that whatever you get by physical aggression costs more than it is worth" (p. 160). He had already expressed this idea in *The League of Frightened Men* (p. 307), but here he describes it as a romantic one. Another instance of Wolfe's romanticism, though he calls it that only indirectly, occurs in *Fer-de-Lance*. District Attorney Anderson's explanation of the Barstow murder is "an offense to truth and an outrage to justice," he explains to Archie, "and since I cherish the one and am on speaking terms with the other, it is my duty to demonstrate to him its inadequacy" (p. 286). When Wolfe demands ten thousand dollars for the solution to the murder Anderson accuses him of being a hijacker. Wolfe denies it: "I have the romantic temperament, but physically I'm not built for it." He is better equipped for another role—finding the cherished truth and demonstrating it.

Wolfe's romanticism provides a motivation for his pursuit of crime and a foundation for the ideology of the Wolfe novels. Wolfe describes himself as "an instrument of vengeance" and compares himself to one of the Greek furies. In order for this self-concept to make sense, there must be some order, the violation of which requires vengeance. If Wolfe merely hired himself out to eke vengeance for individuals, he would be less admirable, a venal servant of a base human urge. The comparison with an Erinys points to the right answer. Like the Furies of Greek myth, Wolfe avenges disruptions of the moral order. He performs his duty for the good of the group, not the individual. The Erinyes took their order from the will of the Gods. The Gods however have gone from twentieth-century New York, so their place is taken by the complex of ideals which Rex Stout described with the conveniently vague label "romantic." In his quest after criminals Wolfe affirms an ideal social order and an ideal personal one. His romanticism lies at the center of the series' appeal.

Wolfe also happens to be a genius. His romanticism supplies Wolfe with a reason to pursue criminals; his genius supplies the tool with which he catches them. If he were merely a romantic, Wolfe would be just another detective; if he were merely a genius, he would be just an extraordinary character. As both, he is a romantic whose idealism is not futile, a genius whose gift is channeled in a specific direction. His role as paid avenger unifies these two elements of Wolfe's character.

The key to Wolfe's genius is that it cannot be explained, studied, or rationalized. It is a thing unto itself. If his genius can be compared to anything, it would be the inspiration of an artist. To emphasize this fact, Wolfe uses the two nouns interchangeably. In *Fer-de-Lance* Wolfe tells Maria Maffei that "there is something in me that can help you; it is genius (p. 12). Later he tells Archie, "I am an artist" (p. 62). In *The League of Frightened Men* Wolfe declares, "I have genius or nothing" (p. 17); later in the novel he alters the phrase to "I am an artist or nothing," a phrase he repeats in *The Red Box* (pp. 190 and 44 respectively). But he draws this connection most emphatically in *Fer-de-Lance*. Archie has been pestering him to explain how he determined the manner of Barstow's death:

> Must I again remind you, Archie, of the reaction you would have got if you had asked Velasquez to explain why Aesop's hand was resting inside his robe instead of hanging by his side? Must I again demonstrate that while it is permissible to request the scientist to lead you back over his footprints, a similar request of the artist is nonsense, since he, like the lark or the eagle, has made none? Do you need to be told again that I am an artist? (pp. 61–62)

Similarly, in explaining to Pete Drossos, a neighborhood child, the elements of detection in *The Golden Spiders*, Wolfe defines detection this way:

> You must thoroughly understand that primarily you are practicing an art, not a science. The role of science in crime detection is worthy, honorable, and effective, but it has little part in the activities of a private detective who aspires to eminence. Anyone of moderate capacity can become adept with a vernier caliper, a camera, a microscope, a spectrograph, or a centrifuge, but they are merely the servants of detection. Science in detection can be distinguished, even brilliant, but it can never replace either the inexorable march of a fine intellect through a jungle of lies and fears to the clearing of truth, or the flash of perception along a sensitive nerve touched off by a tone of a voice or a flicker of an eye.[2]

At the same time that he insists on the artistry of his work, Wolfe firmly rejects the idea that it is in any way unnatural. He permits Fred Durkin in *Fer-de-Lance* to say he has a devil in

him that can find out anything, but he is making allowances for
Durkin's intellect. Later in the novel he reminds Archie, "I am
merely a genius, not a god. A genius may discover the hidden
secrets and display them; only a god could create new ones" (p.
246). In *The Final Deduction* he elevates this disclaimer: "That
would be thaumaturgy, not genius."[3] Wolfe is no miracle worker
in any sense of the phrase. He must issue the same reminder to
Rachael Bruner in *The Doorbell Rang*: "I am neither a thau-
maturge nor a dunce" (p. 7).

Wolfe's own definition of his genius rests on the difference
between phenomena and facts. "I have a feeling for phenomena," he declares in *The Red Box* (p. 40). This "feeling" is one
that Archie does not share, a fact which is responsible for the
division of labor in the Wolfe/Archie relationship: Archie's task
is to garner facts, Wolfe's to interpret phenomena. Wolfe insists
on this distinction in the first novel of the series. When Maria
Maffei first brings her problem—her brother has disappeared—
to Wolfe and Archie, Wolfe begins to question her about the
details of his disappearance: "Where did he—no, no. These are
not phenomena, merely facts. . . . Go on, Archie" (p. 9). Later,
when Archie is fretting over the case, he reflects, "If I undertook
to explain how easy he might be wrong he would just say, 'You
know a fact when you see it, Archie, but you have no feeling for
phenomena'" (p. 65). The most important word in all these discussions seems to be "feels"; the operation of Wolfe's genius is
described not so much in intellectual terms as in intuitive ones.
Wolfe explains this fact to Doctor Bradford: "I had better first
tell you why I have dismissed from my mind the possibility of
your guilt or that of the Barstows. I cannot feel such a guilt. That
is all." Wolfe goes on to give some reasons in support of that
feeling, but they are merely rationalization of an intuition, as he
himself concedes: "That is the rationalization; it is the feeling
that is important" (pp. 173–74).

Thus Wolfe, celebrated for his tough-mindedness, actually
sees himself as a romantic who pursues criminals by intuition.
His genius derives not from his vast reading or his copious knowledge, though these may contribute to it, but rather from his sen-
sitivity to what he calls "phenomena," a term as conveniently
vague as "romantic." From a practical point of view one can see

why Stout would endow Wolfe with this sort of genius; since he never leaves his house on business, relying instead on Archie to bring facts to him, he needs an extra faculty, some sixth sense, to offset his immobility. His "genius" provides that sixth sense and makes his ability to unravel crimes more believable than if he had to know everything secondhand. Furthermore, Wolfe's "genius" is appropriate in a romantic. There is nothing in Wolfe of the tough-guy detective. He is an idealist, and his vision of his own vocation is an exalted one: he demands dignity for his profession. It would be indecorous for such a character to pound the streets the way Sam Spade or even Archie Goodwin would in search of facts. His special province is the intangible. Wolfe is certainly not ethereal—either intellectually or physically—and his grasp of fact can be very sharp indeed. But his genius for phenomena is what sets him apart. Nowhere is this more clear in the Wolfe novels than in *The League of Frightened Men* when Orrie Cather brings in the box that Paul Chapin used to hold discarded items of clothing from a lover who had discarded him. Orrie stands disgusted at what appear to be its trifling contents, and Archie has already told us that "When people begin to get deep and complicated they mix me up" (p. 89). But Wolfe observes, "What we are displaying on this desk-top is the soul of a man" (pp. 136–37). That is a feeling for phenomena.

The third crucial fact about Wolfe is that he is disturbed. His mode of life is a reaction against his vocation, for while he is a romantic, he is also—indeed, cannot help being because of his intelligence—a realist. He is acutely aware of the grimy facts about human order that undercut his romantic conception of it. Indeed his pursuit of crime brings him into constant contact with such reality. He cannot deny it, but he does attempt to escape it in a variety of ways. He tries so hard to escape it that his attempt becomes a form of denial of it. This tension between the ideal and the real pervades the Wolfe series from beginning to end. It is never resolved, never balanced. Instead the romantic vision of the novels gives way to disillusionment and dissonance. The series ends on a disturbing note.

The symptoms of Wolfe's neurosis are evident even as he speaks about his romantic nature. "I suffer," Wolfe says in *Fer-*

de-Lance, "from a romantic conscience" (p. 207); this suspicion
that romanticism is a disease reappears in *Too Many Cooks* where
he describes himself as "an incurable romantic" (p. 119). When
he is not thinking of it as a disease, Wolfe regards romanticism
as an indulgence, a weakness he would like to eradicate. "I wish
I could cure myself of those idiotic romantic gestures," he complains in *Over My Dead Body* (p. 293), and he gives a sense of
the inner tension he feels with his own romantic nature when
he comments in the same novel, "I used to be idiotically romantic. I still am, but I've got it in hand" (p. 134).

It is not clear precisely why Wolfe distrusts his own romantic
temperament, but the novels supply several very likely answers.
One is that ideal conceptions of order, whether of personal or
social order, always have the potential to be wrong. They deal
in areas where there are no absolutes. Thus a paid avenger might
turn out to be in fact nothing more than someone who takes
money for accomplishing someone else's private revenge—a hit
man. If Wolfe should ever find himself in this position, all the
dignity and value would be gone from his vocation. This awareness is not far from Wolfe's consciousness. In the same novel in
which he proclaims himself a hired instrument of vengeance, he
undercuts that claim with this admission: "moral indignation is
a dangerous indulgence. Ethology is a chaos" (p. 178). He speaks
of moral indignation as he would of the romantic temper. Both
are indulgences. Wolfe gives the example of financial banditry.
If we condemn it, who will be a jailer? It is not clear enough
what constitutes financial banditry and what does not—ethology
is a chaos—so who can set up as judge? Yet that is precisely what
Wolfe does in his role as instrument of vengeance. In fact he
makes such decisions every time he accepts a case, for it is well-
known that Wolfe has never had a murderer as a client. Thus
nearly every act of his professional life is potentially an under-
cutting of it.

Over My Dead Body, one of the most bitter of the Wolfe novels, looks back to a time when his romanticism did lead Wolfe
into a false position, and it seems likely that the bitterness of his
tone in this book results from the sense of having chosen wrongly.
"I thought it romantic, when I was a boy, twenty-five years ago,
to be a secret agent of the Austrian government," Wolfe reports

(p. 134), and he refers to this experience as "idiotically romantic."
He has harsh words for the activity of spying itself as well. Part
of Wolfe's doubt about the romantic temper, it seems, stems from
the nagging possibility that he might one day have to look back
on his role as instrument of vengeance with the same regret.

The romantic temper leads Wolfe to an ideal concept of
human nature and society. He abhors violence as beneath human
dignity. He also harbors a vision of the ideal human agreement,
free from racial prejudice. In *Gambit* he declares that "without
dignity man is not a man" and speaks of one's invulnerable loyalty to "his own concept of the obligations of manhood."[4] Yet
these romantic indulgences too are undermined by doubt. In *A
Right to Die*, which, like *Too Many Cooks*, is about the failings
of that ideal human agreement, Wolfe puts his finger on the problem:

> The mind or soul or psyche—take the term you prefer—of any
> man below the level of consciousness is a preposterous mish-
> mash of cesspool and garden.[5]

This being the case, how can his ideals about personal and social
morality be any more than merely ideals? Wolfe sees why an
ideal agreement cannot be reached; at the same time, he cannot
let go of his vision of it.

This awareness of the problematic nature of absolutes leads
directly into the other challenge to Wolfe's romantic temper—
the competing claims of heart and head. John McAleer, in tracing
this issue in Rex Stout's life and in the Wolfe novels, shows that
reason is always trying, and always failing, to control emotion.
Wolfe can easily say, as he does in *The League of Frightened
Men*, that "It is disastrous to permit the vagaries of the heart to
infect the mind" (p. 60), but he can no more succeed in controlling emotion than he can in believing his romantic ideals. As
a result he feels vulnerable. "I carry this fat around to insulate
my feelings," he says in *Over My Dead Body*. "They got too
strong for me once or twice and I had that idea. If I had stayed
lean and kept moving around I would have been dead long ago"
(p. 134). Yet Archie still says, "The only man I know more sensitive than me is Nero Wolfe" (*And Be A Villain*, p. 194). Wolfe,
who does not trust his emotions, cannot suppress them. His "feel-

ing" for phenomena is the essence of his genius, but this sort of feeling, the sort that leads to idiotically romantic gestures and leaves him vulnerable, is also a source of anxiety.

Wolfe's response to the problem of his romantic temper is an avoidance reaction. He stays in his home entirely, except for rare occasions. He sees few people. He binds himself to a rigid daily schedule. He shuns women because of what he perceives as their emotional nature. And he insulates himself with fat. Reading the novels and listening to Archie's narration, it is difficult to think of Wolfe as neurotic, but certainly there is no other way to describe this behavior. Wolfe perceives the sharp discontinuity between the ideal and the real in the world. The contrast produces in him the need to deny the discontinuity by avoiding it, by retreating to his ordered, insulated world. Archie comments perceptively about this mechanism in *A Right to Die*: "You regard anything and everything beyond your control as an insult." Wolfe does not deny the truth of that observation—he merely sharpens it: "Not in nature—only in what men contrive" (p. 32). Wolfe wants to control human behavior in order to preserve his romantic vision.

Wolfe is amazingly candid about the motives for his own disturbed behavior. The principal motive for his seclusion behind walls—of stone and of fat—is his hypersensitivity to people, a hypersensitivity bred by the fact that the closer he gets to people the greater chance there is of a blow to his idealism. In *Fer-de-Lance* he speaks often about seclusion: "unlike most of the persons I avoid meeting by staying inside my house," he tells Anna Fiore, "you are willing to confine your tongue to its proper functions" (p. 26). Archie reports two pages later that Wolfe has "an intense distaste for being touched by anyone," and Wolfe himself admits that "I am too sensitive to strangers, that is why I keep these layers over my nerves" (p. 256).

A specific kind of retreat for which Wolfe is notorious is his misogyny. Actually Wolfe does not hate women. He fears them.[6] When Dina Laszio accuses him of misogyny, he explains:

> Not like women? They are astounding and successful animals. For reasons of convenience, I merely preserve an appearance of immunity which I developed some years ago under the pressure of necessity. (*Too Many Cooks*, p. 151)

Later in the book Marko Vukcic accuses him of hiding "behind a barricade" from women, and Wolfe, sensitive perhaps to the truth of the charge, responds with some harsh words about "decent and intelligent control of the appetites which we share with dogs" (p. 200). Clearly for Wolfe this is a case of trying to control those parts of life that do not fit his romantic mold. He would prefer not to think, for example, that humans share appetites with dogs. His attitude toward women is another form of avoidance.

Wolfe of course does not succeed in withdrawing completely from the chaotic world any more than he succeeds in believing his romantic vision of it. Instead he tries to achieve an equilibrium between the two. As an instrument of vengeance—a detective—he asserts the ideal vision; as a recluse, as a pseudomisogynist, as a fat man, he admits the reality of the chaotic world and attempts to retreat from it. As long as these two visions of the world remain in creative tension with one another, the series goes on, for this tension provides a conflict for the plot, generates interest in the characters, and undergirds the ideology of the series. Wolfe personifies the two greatest competing views of the world—the idealist's and the realist's, the optimist's and the pessimist's, and the working out of the conflict is of universal interest. His particular way of coping with the conflict is unique—Wolfe is nothing if not eccentric—but that very uniqueness generates an interest of a different sort—an interest in character that develops from the series' ideology.

To call Wolfe disturbed is perhaps misleading; finally his neurosis is healthy. Readers of the Wolfe saga year after year see the hero pursuing criminals and bringing them to justice. For him the process may bring disillusionment, but for the reader it affirms and renews the ideal vision. In each novel order is challenged but not destroyed, and one comes away from the story with the pleasure of Wolfe's romantic vision but not the tension of his neurosis. That burden he carries on alone.

7

Archie Goodwin:
Pragmatic Picador

Fundamentally I'm the direct type.
The Red Box

If he has his rules, so do I.
The Second Confession

Outside this house Mr. Goodwin is me, in
effect—if not my alter ego, my vicar.
Gambit

With the possible exception of Holmes and Dr. Watson, Nero
Wolfe and Archie Goodwin form the most successful partnership
in crime fiction. As with Doyle's detectives their partnership is
both domestic and professional, with the difference that the
Wolfe novels tend to emphasize the domestic as much—if not
more—than the professional side of their relationship. With their
interest in menus, schedules, and family bylaws, the Wolfe novels depict not only the pursuit of crime but also the alternative
to the morally disordered world of crime: the excessively ordered
world of the brownstone on West Thirty-fifth Street. That order
depends as much on Archie Goodwin as it does on Nero Wolfe.

Wolfe, especially in the early novels, is a romantic. Archie, by
contrast, is a realist. Wolfe's province is phenomena; Archie's is
facts. Wolfe is subtle; Archie direct. Wolfe's rhetoric verges on
pomposity; Archie's slang is concrete and street-wise. Wolfe
knows who Thales of Miletus was, knows the difference between
the philosophies of Plato and Protagoras, knows all about crisis

intervention in modern psychotherapy. Archie knows who the Mets are, what Off-Track Betting is, where to get pass keys made illegally. This fundamental division of labor enables Wolfe and Archie together to form a complete detecting team, and Archie knows very well how the labor is divided:

> Aside from my primary function as the thorn in the seat of Wolfe's chair to keep him from going to sleep and waking up only for meals, I'm chiefly cut out for two things: to jump and grab something before the other guy can get his paws on it, and to collect pieces of the puzzle for Wolfe to work on. . . . I don't pretend to be strong on nuances. Fundamentally I'm the direct type. (*The Red Box*, p. 180)

Archie makes this point repeatedly, although in slightly different words, throughout the Wolfe novels, but especially towards the beginning of the series when the characters are getting established. Many of his self-revelations occur in comments about food. In *Fer-de-Lance*, Archie misses one of Fritz's special efforts; the next morning Fritz describes what he missed: "I was only politely interested," Archie reports, "yesterday's meals never concern me much" (p. 288). In *And Be A Villain* Wolfe and Fritz are arguing over whether horse mackerel is as good as Mediterranean tunny fish for *vitello tonnato*. Archie listens briefly, until "The argument began to bore me because there was no Mediterranean tunny fish to be had anyhow."[1] In the same trilogy—this time in *In the Best Families*—Archie elaborates punningly on that view: "I fully appreciate, mostly anyhow, the results of Wolfe's and Fritz's powwows on grub when it arrives at the table, but the gab often strikes me as overdone" (p. 16). As a man of action, Archie is not interested in hypothesis or theory, not interested in the unretrievable past or the uncertain future. He is interested in what is on the table, in detecting as well as in dining. He is, as he puts it in *The League of Frightened Men*, a swallower; Wolfe is the taster (p. 130).

Archie's directness springs partly from the attitude that motivates him to detect in the first place. Wolfe pursues criminals to make money, a fact he frankly acknowledges in *Too Many Cooks*, though in the same breath he reminds the reader that he is an incurable romantic. The thrill of the chase motivates Archie, a fact emphasized by his response to the end of Wolfe's relapse

in *Fer-de-Lance*: "I was excited all right. I shaved extra clean
and whistled in the bathtub. With Wolfe normal again anything
might happen," and later, "Fifty grand, with the Wolfe bank balance sagging like a clothesline under a wet horse blanket; and
not only that, but a chance of keeping our places on the platform
in the biggest show of the season" (pp. 90, 91). When Helen Frost
walks in with an important news item in *The Red Box*, Archie's
"heart began to beat, as it always does when we're on a case with
any kick to it and any little surprise turns up" (p. 249). In *Please
Pass the Guilt* Saul Panzer appears on the doorstep with a look
on his face that clearly tells he has cracked the case. Archie opens
up the door: "It's moments like that that make life worth living,
seeing Saul there on the stoop" (p. 130). Where Wolfe's interest
in a case is partly financial, partly romantic, and partly intellectual, Archie's is visceral. As befits the master of fact, the man of
action, for him the appeal of detection is direct and concrete.
Archie feels it in his pulse. No doubt it is this extraordinary bond
between a case and his own physical state that makes Archie so
direct. In fact, he must restrain himself, he is so energized:

> Although I keep it down as much as I can, so it won't interfere
> with my work, I always have an inclination in a case of murder
> to march up to all the possible suspects, one after the other, and
> look them in the eye and ask them, "Did you put that poison in
> the aspirin bottle?" and just keep that up until one of them says,
> "Yes." As I say, I keep it down, but I have to fight it. (*The Red
> Box*, p. 180)

It is as though Archie craved the physical sensation of hearing
that "Yes." The same is true of that suspicion Archie harbors—
though he knows it is false—that if you look hard enough at a
group of murder suspects you can pick out the murderer. It never
works, but he keeps trying.

Wolfe likes a case with complexities. Archie, a great one for
the obvious, does not. "I like a case you can make a diagram of,"
he reports in *And Be A Villain* (p. 129). It is not that he objects
to complications per se; he simply prefers the direct approach
to the circuitous one:

> . . . if you're out for bear it seems silly to concentrate on hunting
> for moose tracks. Our fee depended on our finding out how and

why Orchard got cyanided by drinking Madeline Fraser's sugared coffee, and here we were spending our time and energy on the shooting of a female named Beula Poole. (p. 127)

"I am methodical by temperament," Archie complains elsewhere, and he makes a point of saying that he likes to see plans carried out when they've been made (*Some Buried Caesar*, p. 54). This characteristic serves Archie well as narrator. Wolfe, who closes his eyes and flashes all over a case, all over its facts and phenomena, would be neither prepared for nor disposed towards ordered, detailed narration of a case. That would be like requiring Velasquez to explain how he painted drapery. Archie, however—direct, concrete, methodical—makes an ideal narrator. In watching him come to grips with the case and with Wolfe's artistry, the reader comes to grips with a case as well. Archie is not dull-witted in a Watsonian way; he's simply another sort of detective with another cast of mind than Wolfe.

As the man whose province is facts, Archie periodically punctures Wolfe's romanticism. These occasions—normally comic ones—help keep Wolfe honest. They also keep the Wolfe series active and energetic. Wolfe tends toward laziness; its parallel quality in the moral world is complacency. Fritz once commented to Archie that Wolfe would "do nothing without you to *piquer*" (*The Final Deduction*, p. 28). As picador, Archie keeps Wolfe both physically and mentally alert. In *Fer-de-Lance* Wolfe explains why he allowed E. D. Kimball to be killed. The explanation requires half a page and includes such rhetorical end-runs as "a substitute for fate," "judicial murder," and "the entire complex phenomenon." "I will take the responsibility for my own actions," Wolfe concludes; "I will not also assume the burden of your simplicity" (p. 312). Archie's reply deflates Wolfe's balloon:

> If [the murderer] had been arrested and brought to trial you would have had to put on your hat and gloves, leave the house, walk to an automobile, ride clear to White Plains, and sit around a courtroom waiting for your turn to testify. Whereas now, natural processes being what they are, and you having such a good feeling for phenomena, you can just sit and hold your responsibilities in your lap. (pp. 312–13)

By mocking Wolfe's diction, Archie exposes its underside. Stout is not criticizing Wolfe; he is merely dramatizing the confrontation between a realist and abstractions. In doing so he reveals not only the character of the realist but also the depth of the understanding between his two main characters.

That exchange, though significant, was not particularly amusing. This next one is, in an ironic way. Wolfe and Archie are discussing the taste test that has been arranged for Les Quinze Maîtres and Mrs. Laszio's report of an attempt to murder her husband in *Too Many Cooks*. Wolfe is uneasy. "I came here to meet able men, not to see one or more of them murdered." Archie is not fooled: "You came here to learn how to make sausage" (p. 58). He remembers the conversation with Berin on the train and won't let Wolfe get away with ennobling his own mission. Occurring in the same novel with some of Wolfe's most romantic pronouncements—for example, "The guest is a jewel resting on the cushion of hospitality"—Archie's sardonic realism surely nudges the reader when he hears those grand words. It preserves the thematic direction of the series, for as the remaining novels gradually show, Wolfe's idealism is fated to suffer a severe blow.

Because Archie Goodwin narrates the Wolfe novels the reader sees all the action through his eyes and with his help evaluates all the characters and themes. In fact Rex Stout himself once observed, "It's Archie who really carries the stories, as narrator. Whether the readers know it or not, it's Archie they really enjoy."[2] Being the direct type helps him to fulfill the role of narrator. As he repeatedly remarks, Archie has a straightforward kind of mind. He prefers things clear, direct, methodical. This quality inspires confidence; a reader expects such a narrator to be reliable because of his directness. Archie capitalizes on this fact throughout the Wolfe novels. In *A Right to Die* he states, "I never, in these reports, skimp any step that counts, forward or backward. If I score a point, or if I get my nose pushed in, I like to cover it" (p. 140). In *A Family Affair*, the most intensely personal of their cases, the one where a participant-narrator would be most likely to fudge his account, Archie repeats his assurances: "I try to make these reports straight, straight accounts of what happened, and I'm not going to try to get tricky" (p. 114).

In *Please Pass the Guilt* he reminds the reader again: "in these reports I don't put in stunts to jazz it up, I just report" (p. 81). But Archie's reliability is not really at issue in the point of view of the Wolfe novels. Stout never uses his narrator to offer ambiguous or contradictory versions of reality. Archie's importance as a narrator comes from the values he imposes on the Wolfe saga. It comes as a surprise that Archie, despite his fierce pride, his antiauthoritarian kink, and his roving eye for women is in fact quite rule-bound. He lives by a strict code which he continually alludes to in his reports of Wolfe's cases. His code pervades the novels, giving them an ethical dimension, just as the tension in Wolfe between the romantic and the realist does.

In fact Archie shares that conflict. Where Wolfe is a romantic who constantly brushes up against the real, Archie is a realist who constantly brushes up against the romantic. In *Too Many Cooks* he points out to Wolfe that the real point of the journey was to learn to make sausage. But in the same novel he comes up with this effusion: "You might have thought we were bound for the stratosphere to shine up the moon and pick wild stars" (p. 4). In *Over My Dead Body* Archie permits himself this fancy description: "It was ten to five, and a dingy November dawn was feebly whimpering 'Let there be light,' at my window" (p. 178). Certainly these two passages do not earmark Archie as another Wordsworth, but they show in him an imagination and a verbal fancy which are the bridges to another world beyond that of sidewalk and alleyways.

For the most part, though, Archie resists the transcendent. The best example of this trait is his distrust of the pastoral. In *Too Many Cooks* he reacts this way to the sublime West Virginia mountains:

> I strolled along carefree. There was lots of junk to look at if you happened to be interested in it—big clusters of pink flowers everywhere on bushes which Odell had said was mountain laurel, and a brook zipping along with little bridges across it here and there, and some kind of wild trees in bloom, and birds and evergreens and so on. That sort of stuff is all right, I've got nothing against it, and of course out in the country like that something might as well be growing or what would you do with all the space, but I must admit it's a poor place to look for excitement. Compare

it, for instance, with Times Square or the Yankee Stadium. (p. 40)

This is the realist, the man of action, the direct type who craves excitement from the pursuit of crime. Such a person, one expects, when he does talk about rules will discuss them with a sharp focus on the concrete, the actual. In Archie's case, exactly that happens. On the surface his rules are comic. In *The Second Confession*, for example, he plays off Wolfe's corpulence: "If he has his rules, so do I, and one of mine is that a three-by-four private elevator with Wolfe in it does not need me too, so I took the stairs" (p. 12). In *The Doorbell Rang*, Archie turns interior decorator: "I have a test for people with rooms that big . . . the pictures on the walls. If I can tell what they are, okay. If all I can do is guess, look out; these people will bear watching" (p. 66). *Death of a Doxy* sets down another rule—very practical but not comic: "Because of a regrettable occurrence some years back, I made it a hard and fast rule never to go on an errand connected with a murder without a gun . . ." (p. 44). In *A Family Affair* Archie introduces another rule: "No hat before Thanksgiving. Rain or snow is good for hair" (p. 49). Like Wolfe's inflexible plant schedule and dining hours, these rules are funny because their propagators hold to them so tenaciously even though the rules themselves are trivial or comic or cranky. Yet like Wolfe's rules, which are part of his attempt to impose some regularity and order on careless, scattered reality, Archie's rules point to more important considerations, for many of them are both serious and significant.

In *Fer-de-Lance* Archie's mock-Puritanism was comic. But another rule is not. He explains that Wolfe had a warning bell installed at his bedroom door not out of cowardice but out of his "intense distaste for being touched by anyone or being compelled without warning to make any quick movements." The question of cowardice arises because "ordinarily if I have cause to suspect that a man is yellow as far as I'm concerned he can eat at another table" (p. 30). In *The Red Box* Archie slaps Assistant District Attorney Matthias R. Frisbie for calling Wolfe "underhanded." "In a way I suppose it was all right, and of course it was the only thing to do under the circumstances, but there was no deep satisfaction in it. . . . It had been a fleeting pleasure to smack him . . . but now that it was over there was an inclination inside of me to feel righteous, and that made me glum and in a worse temper than before" (pp. 264–65). *And Be A Villain* offers another rule: "Money may be everything, but it makes a difference how you get it" (p. 105). In *A Right to Die* Wolfe has all the members of ROCC at his office after dinner, but none will accept a drink at first. Archie points out: "It couldn't have been because of my manners, offering to serve people of an inferior race. First, two of them were white, second, when I consider myself superior to anyone, as I frequently do, I need a better reason than his skin" (pp. 76–77).

Archie is a moralist. His rules, expressed or implied, comic or serious, articulate an ethical position. Wolfe, who cannot suppress his belief in an ideal order, tries to achieve that order in part through the constraints of his own schedule. Archie—less imaginative but more realistic—feels that ideal order only intuitively. He compensates for that fact by imposing it more strongly on his own life. Believing perhaps that "the rules you make yourself are the hardest to break" (*Death of a Doxy*, p. 44), he constructs a world of action as firmly bound by rules as Wolfe's contemplative world is bound by his timetable. Archie's method—more concrete and more practical than Wolfe's—ultimately serves the same purpose: to impose an ideal order on messy experience.

In *Fer-de-Lance* Archie assures Sarah Barstow, "you can regard me as Nero Wolfe" (p. 157). Twenty-eight years later in *Gambit* Wolfe assures Mrs. Blount, "Outside this house Mr. Goodwin is me in effect—if not my alter ego, my vicar" (p. 138). These two statements suggest one reason for the close bond between Wolfe and Archie. Wolfe never leaves the house on business, so in order to do any detecting he needs an extension of himself to go around for him. That accounts for Archie's phenomenal memory too, for it enables Wolfe to hear as well as see events at which he is not present.

But the two statements just quoted hint at a far more important link between Wolfe and Archie than the one required by the mechanics of the detective novel. In an important way Archie is

Wolfe's alter ego, not merely his vicar. On the psychological level, their bond rests quite simply on mutual trust and respect. Wolfe explains it in *Too Many Women*:

> Archie. If I need to tell you, I do, that I have unqualified confidence in you and am completely satisfied with your performance in this case as I have been in all past cases and expect to be in all future ones. Of course you tell lies and so do I, even to clients when it seems advisable, but you would never lie to me nor I to you in a matter where mutual trust and respect are involved.[3]

"Respect" is the key word here. Archie needs to have Wolfe's respect and the satisfaction of having earned it; Wolfe's pride is more absolute, a combination of confidence and self-satisfaction. Their mutual pride is their strongest bond, the point at which they merge and their personalities become one. Mortified at having allowed Clyde Osgood to be murdered in the very pasture he was guarding in *Some Buried Caesar*, Archie puts his finger on the link:

> You're accustomed to feeling pleased because you're Nero Wolfe, aren't you? All right, on my modest scale I permit myself a similar feeling about Archie Goodwin. When did you ever give me an errand that you seriously expected me to perform and I didn't perform it? (p. 70)

In *Fer-de-Lance* when he momentarily suspects that assistant district attorney Derwin has tricked him, Archie groans, "If I let a third-rate brief-shark do that to me I'd never be able to look Wolfe in his big fat face again" (p. 52). In *The Second Confession* after Louis Rony switches glasses and gives Archie a drugged bourbon, Archie—still hung over—vows, "He would pay for that or I'd never look Nero Wolfe in the face again" (p. 36). As Wolfe explains to the Sperlings later, "Mr. Goodwin was mortified, and he is not one to take mortification lightly" (p. 234). But Wolfe too feels the prick of pride. In *A Family Affair* he informs Cramer, "I intend to find the man who did it and bring him to account, with the help of Mr. Goodwin, whose self-esteem is as wounded as my own" (p. 48). In giving instructions to Orrie, Saul, and Fred, he vows, "I would like to come out of this with my self-esteem intact" (p. 65). And in the pessimistic mode with which this novel ends he tells Cramer, "Archie told me what Pierre had said when he arrived. . . . Perhaps it was my self-esteem that made me give that item too little thought; Pierre said I was the greatest detective in the world. All is vanity" (p. 147).

But Wolfe and Archie are united by more than a shared sense of pride, just as more than pride motivates their pursuit of crime. Archie is Wolfe's alter ego in another important respect: their shared values. In *A Doorbell Rang* Wolfe needs to play both ends against the middle. To satisfy Cramer he needs to identify the murderer of David Althaus and to hand him over; to satisfy Mrs. Bruner he needs to identify the murderer, and, if he was an FBI man, *not* hand him over. As Archie points out, "Cramer wouldn't like that, that's not his idea at all. Neither would you, really. Making a deal with a murderer isn't your style" (p. 58). Wolfe grunts. "I don't like your pronouns." Archie's reply is important: "All right, make it 'we' and 'us.' It's not my style either." In *Death of a Doxy* Archie again has to revise his pronouns. Speaking of Orrie Cather, who is being held for the murder of Isabel Kerr, he comments, "While he is no Saul Panzer, for years he has come in very handy for you—okay, for us" (p. 19). Forced by circumstances—Wolfe won't leave the house, Archie is not a genius—they function as one detective, one person. As a corporate personality they share the same dominant personality trait—pride. As a corporate ethical center they share the same "style." This is the depth and strength of their bond.

In the first Wolfe novel, where he and Wolfe still seem to be getting to know each other, Archie feels dissatisfied by the conclusion of the case. Wolfe permits a man to be murdered at the end of *Fer-de-Lance* just as he permits the murderer to kill himself rather than surrender to the police. This upsets Archie, who rejects all of Wolfe's self-justification at the end of the case. This sort of conflict occurs rarely in the novels. Normally Wolfe and Archie reach instinctive and unanimous agreement over the moral issues of any event. In *A Family Affair* as soon as Archie and Saul identify the murderer they know what must happen; the only question is how to make it happen. In *Death of a Doxy* when Orrie has been named as a murder suspect Wolfe declares that if he is guilty they should not intervene—"Sympathy with

misfortune, certainly, but not contravention of Nemesis"—and
no one demurs (p. 24). Later in the novel, Wolfe, Fred, Saul, and
Archie display unanimity on the subject of blackmail. Wolfe and
Archie agree on other subjects as well. In *The Doorbell Rang*
they agree about the FBI's overreaching its prerogatives. In *The
Second Confession* they both condemn communism. In *Too
Many Cooks* and *A Right to Die* both despise racism. Perhaps
the best measure of their concord appears at the end of *The Red
Box*, two years after *Fer-de-Lance*. There too Wolfe allows the
murderer to commit suicide. Instead of protesting Archie sits
quietly, marveling at the murderer's composure in swallowing
poison before a crowd of unsuspecting observers.

And so in the end Archie proves both very like and very different from Wolfe. He possesses a different cast of mind from
Wolfe's, preferring the direct to the subtle, the concrete to the
ideal. Insofar as he and Wolfe rub up against each other, these
differences produce comedy, as they do when Archie deflates
Wolfe's rhetoric or chastises his inactivity. But these differences,
far from driving the two characters apart, actually bring them
together, for it is through these differences that Wolfe and Archie
complement each other. Underneath them rests a broad base of
similarity. Wolfe and Archie share tremendous pride, a force that
motivates them to pursue some crimes and, once they have
begun, to solve others. That pride is the twin of a shared moral
code which operates in the ethical sphere as their pride does in
another sphere to hold Wolfe and Archie together. In their shared
obsession with rules, timetables, schedules, Wolfe and Archie
attempt to recreate in the messy real world the ideal order they
envision. Their obsession reinforces their solidarity and gives
their quest substance and meaning.

8

The Thirty-Fifth Street Irregulars

Nero Wolfe and Archie Goodwin dominate the Wolfe novels. Intriguing and appealing as individuals, they merge over the course of the saga to form a greater whole—both as a crime-fighting team and as a personality. Taken together they are both active and contemplative, romantic and realistic, cerebral and physical. Together they reconcile two traditions in crime fiction and two ways of looking at the world.

But they do not operate alone. Try as he might to insulate himself from the world, even Wolfe must interact with other people besides Archie. One of them is his chef, Fritz Brenner. In terms of the structure of the Wolfe novels, Fritz occupies an ambiguous position. On the one hand, he functions as an insulator, preserving the sealed world Wolfe has constructed for himself. On the other hand, as the chef who entertains visitors with cooking—"the subtlest and kindliest of the arts," as Wolfe calls it (*Too Many Cooks*, p. 163)—and as the one who frequently ushers in callers, Fritz constitutes a link with the outside world just as Archie does.

Like Wolfe, Fritz does not like having women in the house. Archie describes his attitude and manner this way in *Over My Dead Body*:

> He was stiffly formal, as was his invariable custom when there were ladies present, not from any sense of propriety but from fear. Whenever any female, no matter what her age or appearance, got inside the house, he was apprehensive and ill at ease until she got out again. (p. 126)

Similarly, in *Death of a Doxy*, Archie remarks to Fritz, "There is one man who is more allergic to a woman in this house than he [Wolfe] is, and you are it" (p. 142).

Fritz's gynephobia, according to Archie, springs from his fear that since he performs traditionally feminine tasks in the home, any woman who enters the brownstone may supplant him by taking on these tasks herself. (This happens, incidentally, in *Black Orchids*, when Maryella Timms actually takes over the kitchen to show Wolfe how to use fresh pig chitlins in corned beef hash.) Clearly Fritz has less to fear from women whose appeal is sexual than from those whose appeal is maternal, for Fritz is really a mother rather than a wife. He emphatically rejects a wife's role in *Too Many Women*. Archie comes down for breakfast to find fresh oatmeal, cream, eggs, ham, pancakes, and steaming coffee. "I made a pass as if to kiss him on the cheek, he kept me off with a twenty-inch pointed knife" (pp. 140–41). At the same time, the novels reinforce the identification of Fritz with Archie's mother. In *Death of a Doxy* Archie watches Fritz make head cheese to see why Fritz's is so much better than his mother's; in *The Final Deduction* Archie's mother writes glowingly of Fritz's chestnut croquettes, and throughout the novels Fritz displays a maternal concern for the comfort and safety of the two men under his roof.

Whatever the reasons for Fritz's gynephobia, the significant fact is that it makes him an insulator for Wolfe. Fritz—especially in Archie's absence—guards the two entrances to the brownstone, the front door and the telephone. The telephone he often simply will not answer. Occasionally he will not answer the door, but more often he leaves the chain bolt on and peers out the two-inch crack it allows—a perfect image of the defender of the castle. On rare occasions Fritz is even a defender of the castle within the castle, as in *Death of a Doxy* when he camps outside Julie Jaquette's bedroom with a vacuum cleaner to keep her there as long as Avery Ballou is in the house.

In crime fighting however Fritz becomes a eunuch figure. He shares with Wolfe and Archie a deep concern for the domestic arrangements of the brownstone; unlike them his concerns do not mirror a world view. Fritz is not a crime fighter, but he has other roles, unlike Theodore Horstman, Wolfe's "orchid nurse," who is insignificant because his concerns extend only to flowers, not at all to people. So if the walls of Wolfe's brownstone are Fritz's desmesne they are also his boundary; his concerns extend no further. His function complements Cramer's, for Cramer is concerned only with the world outside the brownstone, the world of crime, and not the inner world—"Your goddam household squabbles will keep," as he rudely says in *Too Many Women* (p. 122). For Fritz, household squabbles will not keep—they are his world. When Wolfe inexplicably disappears in *In the Best Families*, Fritz's first thought is, "Where will he sleep? What will he eat?" (p. 63). A minute later he has gotten only as far as "What is it, Archie? . . . His appetite has been good" (p. 64). Outside of his protecting and mothering role, Fritz is helpless.

Inspector Cramer of Manhattan Homicide is rarely helpless. In the Wolfe novels he appears to be a blocking character, for in nearly every case he undertakes, sooner or later Wolfe finds himself battling Cramer. In at the beginning of a case and in at the end, Cramer shouts, bullies, splutters, and hurls unsmoked cigars. He threatens to jail Wolfe, to take away his license, to catch him in a colossal blunder; yet, he succeeds at none of these. He does however do one thing superlatively well—he helps Wolfe solve crimes.

Archie cannot precisely define their relationship with Cramer. In *And Be A Villain* Archie notes, "He called me Archie only when he wanted to peddle the impression that he regarded himself as one of the family, which he wasn't" (p. 102). In *A Right to Die* Cramer is a man "whom I couldn't exactly call an enemy and wouldn't presume to call a friend" (p. 42). In *Death of a Doxy* he calls Cramer, "An old pal of ours. In reverse" (p. 146). Wolfe has a similar difficulty. In *The Doorbell Rang* he comments acidly, "I wouldn't have thought . . . that Mr. Cramer could be such an ass" (p. 58). Yet in *A Family Affair* he avows to Cramer, "I respect your integrity, your ability, and your understanding. I even trust you up to a point." (p. 99).

For all his huffing and puffing Cramer does go out of his way to help Wolfe in his biggest cases. He tells them about the Althaus murder in *The Doorbell Rang*; he makes a special trip to the brownstone to try to keep Wolfe out of jail in *A Family Affair*; he tries to warn Wolfe about Zeck in *In the Best Families*. But

he does not help solve crimes this way, for these are conscious
acts and his principal virtue is an unconscious one. Archie points
it out:

> Also in my book there was the idea that I had once mentioned
> to him [Wolfe], the idea that it took a broil with Inspector Cramer
> to wind him up. Of course when I had offered it, he had fired
> me or I had quit, I forget which. But I hadn't dropped the idea.
> (*Please Pass the Guilt*, p. 63)

Like Archie, Cramer goads Wolfe. He competes with him. In fact
by his very position and personality he plays on Wolfe's most
prominent personality trait—his pride. Wolfe takes great pleasure in unmasking criminals before an audience which includes
Cramer, in saying, "Mr. Cramer is here only as an observer."
Wolfe pays Archie, as he often remarks, to goad him into action,
and Archie does this well. But once the case is under way, it is
Cramer whose periodic visits fan the flame, who keeps Wolfe
going by bumping into him. Cramer is not a Lestrade. He is
neither ignorant nor foolish, a fact which explains Archie's am-
bivalence towards him despite their frequent and hostile encounters. He would not have earned Wolfe's and Archie's respect
and affection if his role in the novels were primarily negative.
    Cramer serves a function opposite from Fritz's. He brings
the outside world into Wolfe's house while Fritz keeps it out.
On the other hand, he too preserves Wolfe's seclusion. Cramer
conforms to Wolfe's plant and meal schedules. He does not expect Wolfe to come down to his offices. Certainly he does not
mother Wolfe or Archie, but he does finally accept their version
of order. As a policeman he subscribes to the same values as
Wolfe and Archie. Hard-boiled detective stories often portray the
detective as a crusader for truth pitted against corrupt policemen,
so that the antagonism between cop and hero becomes a moral
one. This does not happen in the Wolfe novels. The only time
Archie even approaches an accusation of this kind, Cramer tries
to knock him down. Classical crime fiction often portrays the
police as inept, so that the antagonism between detective and
policeman becomes intellectual. The Wolfe novels toy with this
tradition but finally reject it. Wolfe and Cramer respect each other's intellects and moral codes. In a way then Cramer is part of

the family after all, despite Archie's earlier comment. He subscribes to their code and functions as a goad rather than a hindrance. An important part of the Wolfe saga, Cramer helps to create its intensity and emphasize its final order.

Saul Panzer, Fred Durkin, and Orrie Cather are members of the family. Archie refers to them as family twice in *Too Many Women* (pp. 147 and 167), and they speak of themselves as family members in the important scene of *A Family Affair* where Wolfe plots his strategy to catch the murderer of Pierre Ducos. Most of the Wolfe novels offer capsule descriptions of the three freelancers. Saul, whom Wolfe prefers to the other two, Archie describes as "two inches shorter, much less presentable with his big ears and unpressed pants, and in some ways smarter than me" (*A Family Affair*, p. 63). Everyone who has read the Wolfe novels knows about Saul's preeminence. Fred and Orrie are more complicated:

> Fred was some bigger than Orrie. When he did anything at all, walk or talk or reach for something, you always expected him to trip or fumble, but he never did, and he could tail better than anybody I knew except Saul, which I could never understand. Fred moved like a bear, but Orrie like a cat. Orrie's strong point was getting people to tell him things. It wasn't so much the questions he asked. As a matter of fact, he wasn't very good at questions; it was just the way he looked at them. Something about him made people feel he ought to be told things. (*The Second Confession*, pp. 168–69)

Saul is flawless; Fred and Orrie, by contrast, each do a particular thing well. In a sense each represents a type of detective. Fred resembles the hard-boiled detective, big and physical. Orrie belongs to the same type as Archie—the smooth, handsome ladies' man. Saul most closely resembles the gentleman detective. He plays the piano, quotes Oscar Wilde, flies an airplane. Detecting could almost be an avocation for him.

Yet even though they derive from recognizable types, Saul, Fred, and Orrie—Wolfe's professional family—exist autonomously as characters. They are more than detectives, they are people. Fred is shy, fumbling, slow, loyal. In *A Family Affair* everyone has a martini; "Fred didn't like the taste of gin but he wanted to be sociable" (p. 90). In *The Second Confession* Fred

drinks beer though he prefers bourbon because of "the notion
that he would offend Wolfe if he didn't take beer when invited"
(p. 170). In *Death of a Doxy* Fred and Julie Jaquette joke about
Julie taking one of Fred's children. Archie reflects, "Knowing
him, I hoped she didn't think he meant it" (p. 137). Saul Panzer
is a flatter character than Fred because he is so perfect. He almost
never fails, is never embarrassed or out of place, rarely surprised.
To outline his character would be merely to list his talents.

Orrie Cather is an Archie Goodwin without a dedication to
order. Orrie wants Archie's job, as all the family members rec-
ognize in both *Death of a Doxy* and *A Family Affair*. Furthermore, he is like Archie—well-built, handsome, suave. Archie resists comparisons of this kind with Orrie (when Orrie comments,
"I'm not his [Wolfe's] Archie Goodwin," Archie responds, " I
prefer to regard myself as my Archie Goodwin"), but the novels
insist upon them. So in judging their respective behavior the
reader is forced into judgments about both Orrie and Archie.
Finally the novels show that Orrie lacks Archie's common sense,
which operates as a check to his vanity, and his moral impulse.
He is a superficial Archie.

The novels present Orrie in a negative light from the start.
In *Fer-de-Lance* at the prebattle strategy session, Gore and Durkin arrive on time "and Orrie wasn't late enough to matter" (p.
266). Archie implies that Orrie is not quite up to the mark even
here. *The League of Frightened Men* portrays Orrie as insensi-
tive, if not downright thick. He brings Paul Chapin's box but
utterly fails to understand either its importance or its pathos.
Ironically Orrie puts a finger on his own shortcoming in *The
Second Confession*. On the subject of a conscience, he tells Fred,
"I'm too sophisticated to have one" (p. 171). *Death of a Doxy*,
though, discusses Orrie most thoroughly, and here the weaknesses hinted at before become stated. Wolfe finds him vexing,
Saul finds him pushy, Archie does not trust him, and even Fritz
would rather have him in trouble than any of the others.

As cogs in the machine of the Wolfe novels, Saul, Fred, and
Orrie have several important functions. Like Archie and Cramer,
they act as conduits through which the outside world reaches
into Wolfe's retreat to engage him in its concerns. At the same
time, like Archie and Cramer and Fritz, they help preserve that

retreat by conforming to its rules. Together with Archie, they make it possible for Wolfe to remain in the detecting business. They are his arms, legs, eyes, and ears when Archie is occupied or unavailable.

Above all, though, they are members of the family. They share Wolfe's romanticism. They offer to work for nothing in *Death of a Doxy* and *A Family Affair* partly to see justice done, partly to defend the family integrity. They share Wolfe's and Archie's moral impulse in their judgment on characters like Zeck, the murderer in *A Family Affair*, or on a criminal act like blackmail. Standing just off-center in the Wolfe novels, ready to support and defend Archie and Wolfe, they make Wolfe's world seem more probable. He and Archie are not alone, for the three musketeers—as they are once called—stand ready to give muscle to Wolfe's romantic order.

9

Double-Dome on Mean Street: Rex Stout's Place in Crime Fiction

With the publication of *A Family Affair* in 1975, his eighty-ninth year, Rex Stout's literary career came to an end. In a few weeks he would be dead, his ashes scattered over the grounds at High Meadow. Applauded by readers of distinction around the world, honored by mystery writers, buoyed by ever-strong sales of his Nero Wolfe novels, he occupied a preeminent place among crime fiction writers even before his passing. An analysis of his achievement today therefore must go beyond these outward signs of success, for the true extent of his accomplishment cannot be measured merely in terms of sales or awards.[1] It appears instead in his contribution to crime fiction as a genre.

Rex Stout did more than write very fine mystery novels; he permanently altered the course of crime fiction by showing how it was possible to combine the two separate traditions—those of the hard-boiled op and the Great Detective—which had comprised the genre before him. At the same time he helped advance the place of the mystery novel among the genres of fiction by bringing it closer to the novel of manners. He showed how the crime novel could broaden its scope and its pretensions. He helped bring it into the mainstream of fiction.

In the Nero Wolfe novels Stout created a world of characters, places, and ideas so fully imagined that it can accommodate far more than just the crime plot. It is a proving ground for character, a battleground of ideas, a school of manners. This capacity for depth makes his vision mature. None of the other great American crime writers, and few of the European ones, can boast so many novels of such high quality written over so long a period of time. Through his incisive play of mind and bright, clean prose, he held and satisfied readers around the world—and continues to do so today.

As others have already observed, Rex Stout made a great contribution to crime fiction when he put Nero Wolfe and Archie Goodwin in the same office.[2] *Fer-de-Lance* marks the merger of crime fiction's two principal traditions, the beginning of a new richness and diversity for the genre. Traditionally there have been two kinds of detectives—the hard-boiled detective and the classical one, each presiding over his own branch of the crime novel. The hard-boiled detective, exemplified in American fiction by Spade and Marlowe and alive today in Robert B. Parker's Spenser, boasts good looks, quick fists, a gun he is not afraid to shoot, and an equally deadly weapon of sardonic wit that spurs and goads suspects throughout the novel. He spends his time on the streets, solving crimes by interrogating, chasing, often brawling; as often as not he ends up wounded himself. His arena is the city, especially Los Angeles or New York. His weaknesses are women and alcohol. The Great Detective, descended from Poe's Dupin and typified by Sherlock Holmes, is a different sort. His kingdom is his study and his weapons are intellectual—logic, memory, concentration. He traps criminals in the corridors of his own mind rather than in a back alley at midnight. He is a cultivated gentleman, whose recreation is the library, whose background is often European.

Archie, even with all his glib sophistication, is at heart a hard-boiled type. He chases, punches, shoots, breaks and enters. He knows locksmiths, cabbies, doormen. Wolfe occupies the other extreme. What in other detectives of his school is a preference for the study in him becomes a positive abhorrence of life outside his front door. What in others is a talent for deduction becomes in him inspired genius. By rights, Archie belongs in a run-down neighborhood pounding on doors, Wolfe in a country house quizzing a butler.

But Rex Stout put them both in an office on West Thirty-fifth Street. Such a combination opened vast possibilities for the development of plot, character, and theme in the crime novel. Take plot, for example. The hard-boiled novel is fast-paced and lean; the classical crime novel, on the other hand, is contemplative, intricate, sophisticated. The partnership between Wolfe and Archie allowed for novels which were both fast-paced and contemplative, both lean and sophisticated. Able to modulate between scenes in Wolfe's office and scenes on the street, between Archie tailing someone and Wolfe logomachizing, Rex Stout elaborated the rhythm and pace of the crime novel. He does not have to rely upon one startling event near the close of each chapter—the monotonous build, climax, build, climax rhythm of so much crime fiction. The rhythm of his novels, although still keyed to the development of plot, is less melodramatic. He is able to open or close a chapter with Archie doing something dramatic or Wolfe doing something dramatic. But since Wolfe's drama is usually produced by an act of mind and Archie's by some physical heroics, the drama can be either one of intensity or one of movement. The result is more varied rhythm.

This partnership also had advantages for characterization. The partnership of the two detectives is like a marriage between two strong-willed people: the two kinds are bound to rub against each other. But the resulting tensions, far from rocking the novels, contribute to the richness of texture that Rex Stout contributed to the mystery novel. He managed to join the two types without completely destroying the integrity of either. This left him with all the rough edges between two very different personalities to graft on to his subject. The relationship between the two detectives thus becomes one of his novels' most important subjects, and character and dialogue become correspondingly more important. The novels' events, still shocking, frustrating, exciting, and finally rewarding, are now distanced and highlighted by the intricately patterned personal relations between the two detectives. Wolfe and Archie bicker and badger their way through their cases, alternately pleased and disgusted by each other. This byplay affords the best perspective on the mystery novel, one where the business of fighting crime is seen through the complex domestic staging of the Wolfe-Archie relationship that gives the novels a broader interest and a wider range.

His attempt to combine the two kinds of crime fiction in the Nero Wolfe novels leaves Stout open to criticism. With their amusing, interesting, and often edifying byplay, Wolfe and Archie often distract from the actual case at hand. While their office and dinner conversation is rarely irrelevant to the concerns of the novel, its connection can be tangential. They may argue about how to dispose of a murderer or how to approach one; however they are just as likely to argue over the truth of one of Wolfe's aphorisms, such as his observation that answering letters is a "mandate of civility." Discussions of what constitutes "civility" are not irrelevant to crime fiction, but neither are they immediately relevant to the question of who killed Mrs. X. In his essay on the mystery novel in *The Writer's Book* Stout had argued that the detective "is and must be the hero" of the detective novel and that while "It is permissible to get the reader interested, if you can, in the difficulties and dexterities of the other characters, those concerns must always be tangential."[3] Was he not committing the related mistake of getting the reader too interested in his detectives?[4]

There are two answers to this criticism. One is that of John McAleer, who calls such a view a "heresy." It signifies, he says, "a failure to come to grips with the essence of the characters themselves. Wolfe and Archie actually are extensions of their creator, and both relate intimately to his intrapsychic life." Rex Stout used Wolfe and Archie, both of whom bear important resemblances to their creator, in his own search for self-understanding. Their domestic order and stability mirrors the one Stout himself achieved, and it implies a model of social order and stability. Thus the byplay between Wolfe and Archie makes important connections between the inner world of their creator and the ethos of the whole Wolfe saga. The other answer is offered in Chapter 2 of this book. Even if we knew nothing of Rex Stout's own search for order we would have the evidence of the Wolfe novels. That search is their real subject. The pursuit of crime and the pursuit of romantic order in the brownstone on West Thirty-fifth Street merge and become the same quest. The attempt to separate any particular case Wolfe and Archie investigate from their interrelationship with their environment and the relationship with each other is invidious.

Important changes within a genre prompt corresponding changes
in the relations between that genre and other forms of writing.
As crime fiction became richer and more complex with Rex Stout,
its place among the other genres altered too. It moved further in
the direction towards which, since its inception, it had inevitably
tended—towards the mainstream of fiction. Stout's contribution
to this process deserves emphasis: he helped to attach the crime
novel to mainstream fiction at a particular point—the novel of
manners.

At its core the crime novel, especially the hard-boiled novel,
has often and unfortunately been an adventure story. Its purpose
has been to relate an exciting chase. It asks the simple question,
"Whodunit?" While it functions only at this level, the crime
novel can never approach the mainstream of fiction because it
is restricted merely to relating events rather than to exploring
their significance. It approaches the mainstream to the degree
to which it goes beyond the question of whodunit. There are
many ways to do this. One is to explore problems such as why
the crime was committed, why someone felt the need to catch
the villain, and how crime and catching criminals connects with
the social order. As it explores these questions the crime novel
drifts towards the psychological novel, the sociological novel, or
the mythic novel. The crime novel has developed in all these
directions, and even the Wolfe novels show an interest in psychology and sociology. But Rex Stout took the other way to get
beyond whodunits. Sensing that the best method would be one
that offered the most potential for diversity, he avoided pinning
his novels to one kind of approach, such as the psychological.
Instead he pinned them to a particular way of portraying character and action: the novel of manners.

The novel of manners portrays people in social situations such
as dinner parties, at-homes, or casual conversations, studying
their behavior and implicitly commenting on what it reveals
about their beliefs and values. From the seemingly insignificant
manners it paints, this kind of novel draws important conclusions
about people and society. Its greatest exponent is Jane Austen,
one of Rex Stout's favorite authors, who brilliantly dissects the
minds and hearts of a wide variety of characters even though she
confines her novels to two or three families in small country

villages.[5] Though they portray life in intimate societies, her novels, in probing the meaning of those lives, actually reflect on the great puzzle of human behavior everywhere.

At first glance the crime novel seems an unlikely candidate for the same genre with Jane Austen. Yet Rex Stout consistently reveals in his novels an interest in character, personal relations, and their underlying issues.

No one has done more with character in crime fiction than Rex Stout. The characters of Wolfe and Archie—and to a lesser extent those of the rest of their circle—are the glory of the Wolfe saga. These novels are not only about catching criminals—they are about vanity and our strategies for preserving self-esteem both among our friends and among our enemies, about habit, intellectual styles, humor as a weapon and a defense, about sentiment in conflict with cynicism, realism boring at idealism, about independence in conflict with authority. They portray moral indignation, sincerity, conviction. They portray frivolity, exuberance, wit.

This holds not only for the main characters but for the minor ones as well. Rex Stout's world was populated not only by Wolfe and Archie but also by Cramer, Saul Panzer, Fred and Orrie, Fritz and Theodore, and Lily Rowan, as well as the gallery of memorable characters who appear in individual novels, from Paul Chapin to Julie Jaquette. The criminals one meets in the Wolfe saga offer portraits of bombast, greed, trickery, obsession, seduction and betrayal. The minor characters of the Wolfe circle act as foils for Wolfe and Archie, highlighting their personalities and their values.

Again Rex Stout's critics will argue that he invested too heavily in character in the Wolfe novels, that he ended up writing not crime fiction but simply a watered-down version of "serious" fiction, that he should have focused more sharply on the crime or given up writing crime fiction. *The League of Frightened Men*, such critics will argue, spends enormous amounts of time investigating and discussing Paul Chapin's bizarre emotional life only to show that he was not the murderer after all.[6] Stout's interest in psychology, a holdover from his days as a serious novelist, warped *The League of Frightened Men*. Such criticism is valid if one grants its premise: that crime fiction should be about the investigation of a crime and nothing else. Such a view, though, trivializes the genre, and Rex Stout's Nero Wolfe novels have been so successful precisely because they do the opposite: they enrich the genre.

Few crime fiction writers have been as amusing as Rex Stout. His humor also marks his affinity with the novel of manners, for that genre characteristically portrays human behavior with a lightness of tone which counterpoints its serious undertone of moral criticism. That lightness Rex Stout brought into the crime novel. Other narrators before Archie Goodwin had been funny, but their humor was sardonic, mordant, acid. Archie is whimsical. Instead of a grim surface of hard-boiled dialogue which pounds in to the reader the action of the crime novel, Rex Stout offers a surface compounded largely of the inventive and optimistic wit which distances the grim misdeeds committed in the book. Such wit is not discordant; it provides a relief from the grim deeds of the criminals and saves Archie from sounding self-important.

This light tone saves the Wolfe novels from the two great pitfalls of crime fiction: sentimentalism and pomposity. As a genre that seeks out discrepancies between what we think of ourselves and what we really are, between our interpretations of events and the reality of them, the novel of manners cannot usually be fooled into accepting emotion disproportionate to the occasion or facile philosophizing. This delicate balance of tone carries over into the Wolfe novels. No other writer of crime fiction has controlled tone as successfully and consistently as Rex Stout. His novels are serious but not overbearing, light but not frivolous. Their treatment is realistic, their commentary subtle, their tone balanced.

Rex Stout preserved a balanced tone because his vision was mature. His novels are distinguished by the distance they maintain between the author and his detectives. Unlike many crime writers, Rex Stout did not create a character he loved or wanted to be. His portrayal of Wolfe and Archie is not colored by hero-worship, sentiment, self-identification, or self-abasement. His ability to be funny about them shows that he did not take them too seriously. Wolfe is stubborn, petty, and vain, and Archie foppish, sentimental, proud. In viewing his characters objectively, though by no means coldly, Stout avoided the dangers of passing off as heroic behavior that is manifestly unheroic, or of glorifying virtues that are dubious at best. He knew better than to create a detective who was an impossibly perfect man. His treatment is as tough-minded as Wolfe himself could have wished. This tough-mindedness carries over into his handling of plot. The Wolfe novels minimize violence, sex, and melodrama, the hallmarks of cheap crime fiction. As one would expect from a writer who helped move the whole genre away from the whodunit, Rex Stout deemphasized the shoot-out, the vulnerable and pliant female, the tough interrogations in dimly lit rooms. He was a novelist with something more sturdy upon which to base his work—dialogue, character, and setting—and his treatment of the conventions of the genre amply demonstrated that fact.

In evaluating Rex Stout's achievement there is one other fact to keep in mind: he sustained it over forty years. Few writers, and even fewer crime writers, can lay claim to the sustained excellence of Rex Stout's Nero Wolfe novels. To write one book, excellent in its kind, is a difficult achievement. Having done so marks Stout as a writer with a significant enough vision and supple enough mind to please readers over a period of time marked by great political, social, and cultural change. He could discuss World War II or Watergate, civil rights or women's rights, and do so as cogently in his eighty-ninth year as in middle age.

Stout owed his success over forty years not to mercenary reliance on a formula or to callow exploitation of novelty. He simply created a variation of the crime novel that suited him and then elaborated on it. He steadily accumulated over the course of the Wolfe saga enough detailed information about his world and the characters in it so that he had a rich repository of traits and habits, shared with his readers, upon which he could draw at any time to establish links with past novels and to drop hints for future ones. The relation between *Death of a Doxy* and *A Family Affair* is a good case in point. In both of these novels Orrie Cather finds himself in an awkward spot. In both cases the same character trait lands him in trouble. In both cases Wolfe and Archie get involved. The trouble is that one case ends much differently from the other. But the point is that the reader understands Orrie's character well enough to accept and even subconsciously to anticipate the end of the later novel because of what happened in the earlier one. Wolfe's behavior in *A Family Affair* is unprecedented, yet reflection on the principles he has enunciated over and over again in the novels, on his behavior in similar circumstances, and a general knowledge of his character, makes what he does as reasonable as daylight. Archie too behaves in an amazing way in the later novel, but again a little thought about the facts of his character, his relationship with Orrie, his principles, makes his behavior clear. Even the commentary on justice and nemesis in both novels sounds similar because it makes the same point, allowing for the different circumstances of the second novel. *A Family Affair* is certainly not cribbed from *Death of a Doxy*, but in a positive sense it is another version of it. This sort of interconnectedness holds the entire Wolfe series together. It allows for diversity within unity, for development within a pattern—in short, for longevity.

Ultimately this must be the greatest praise of a writer—that he was capable of imagining a world complex enough and yet real enough to interest readers, to supply him with events and characters and themes, and to bear variation and elaboration over so long a period of time. Such sustained achievement is of course a tribute to persistence and to technical skill. Most of all though it must be a tribute to imagination, and it is on the score of his imagination that finally Rex Stout merits our praise and admiration.

Notes

Chapter 1

1. The standard biography is John McAleer, *Rex Stout: A Biography* (Boston: Little Brown, 1977), upon which I depend heavily in this chapter. Hereafter cited as McAleer.
2. McAleer, 75.
3. McAleer, 50–51.
4. McAleer, 43.
5. McAleer, 44.
6. McAleer, 78.
7. McAleer, 122.
8. McAleer, 123.
9. New York: Viking Press, 1977.
10. McAleer, 242.
11. When asked "Why did you start writing detective stories?" Stout replied: "I might write another dozen or even two dozen novels and they would all get pretty good reception but, two things, they wouldn't make any large amount of money and they wouldn't establish me in the first rank of writers. So, since that wasn't going to happen, to hell with sweating out another twenty novels when I'd have a lot of fun telling stories which I could do well and make some money on it. So I did." John McAleer, *Royal Decree: Conversations with Rex Stout* (Ashton, MD: Pontes Press, 1983), 3. Hereafter cited as *Royal Decree.*
12. McAleer, 255.
13. Asked what accounted for his publishing eight books between 1938 and 1940, Stout answered: "Eight books in three years? I'm surprised but not impressed. I must have needed money for something" (*Royal Decree*, 7).

14. McAleer, 307.
15. McAleer, 313–314.
16. McAleer, 314.
17. McAleer, 329–331.
18. *New York Times*, Nov. 29, 1965.
19. McAleer, 498.
20. McAleer, 521.
21. McAleer, 4–5.

Chapter 2

1. McAleer, 371.
2. *The Writer's Book*, ed., Helen Hull (New York: Harper and Brothers, 1950), 63. Hereafter cited parenthetically in the text.

Chapter 3

1. McAleer, 276.
2. See David Anderson, "Crime and Character: Notes on Rex Stout's Early Fiction," *The Armchair Detective*, 13 (Spring, 1980): 169–171.
3. *Fer-de-Lance* (New York: Farrar and Rinehart, 1934), 59.
4. *The League of Frightened Men* (New York: Farrar and Rinehart, 1935), 199.
5. *The Red Box* (New York: Farrar and Rinehart, 1937), 143.
6. *Some Buried Caesar* (New York: Farrar and Rinehart, 1939), 120.

Chapter 4

1. *Over My Dead Body* (New York: Farrar and Rinehart, 1940), 5–6.
2. *The Second Confession* (New York: Viking Press, 1949), 9 and 226.
3. *In the Best Families* (New York: Viking Press, 1950), 111.

Chapter 5

1. McAleer, 520.
2. *The Doorbell Rang* (New York: Viking Press, 1965), 163.
3. *A Family Affair* (New York: Viking Press, 1975), 69.
4. *Please Pass the Guilt* (New York: Viking Press, 1973), 36.
5. *Death of a Doxy* (New York: Viking Press, 1966), 19.

Chapter 6

1. *Too Many Cooks* (New York: Farrar and Rinehart, 1938), 119.
2. *The Golden Spiders* (New York: Viking Press, 1953), 13.
3. *The Final Deduction* (New York: Viking Press, 1961), 30.
4. *Gambit* (New York: Viking Press, 1962), 177 and 41.
5. *A Right to Die* (New York: Viking Press, 1964), 40.
6. Wolfe has often been accused of latent homosexuality. See McAleer, 268–9.

Chapter 7

1. *And Be a Villain* (New York: Viking Press, 1948), 9.
2. McAleer, 282.
3. *Too Many Women* (New York: Viking Press, 1947), 122.

Chapter 9

1. "Obviously the books I've written have got something in them that distinguishes them from the ordinary run of books—obviously or there wouldn't be all these goddam articles and things, and I wouldn't get all these letters. What I don't know is what the books have in them that lots of books don't have. . . . I'm just curious as to what in hell it is that, in so far as they are, makes them at all distinctive" (*Royal Decree*, 72–73).
2. See McAleer, 5–6.
3. See 18 above.
4. This was one of the criticisms of Stout leveled by the celebrated man of letters Edmund Wilson, who complained of both *The League of Frightened Men* and *The Red Box* that "they were full of long episodes that led nowhere and had no real business in the story." "Why do People Read Detective Stories?" in Edmund Wilson, *A Literary Chronicle 1920–1950* (Garden City, NY: Doubleday & Company, Inc., n.d.), Doubleday Anchor Books, 325. The essay first appeared in *The New Yorker*, 20 (October 14, 1944), 73–75. Of course, Wilson disliked most crime fiction. See "Who Cares Who Killed Roger Ackroyd?" in the same volume.
5. For Stout's admiration of Jane Austen see McAleer, 252, 291, 441, 495, 557.
6. Wilson said of the novel: "With Nero Wolfe—though *The League of Frightened Men* makes use of a clever psychological idea—the

solution of the mystery was not usually either fanciful or unexpected. I finally got to feel that I had to unpack large crates by swallowing the excelsior in order to find at the bottom a few bent and rusty nails." But he also said that Stout, unlike Agatha Christie, "has made some attempt at characterization of the people that figure in crimes." (*A Literary Chronicle*, 325 and 326).

Selected Bibliography

Note: Readers requiring complete bibliographical information should consult Guy M. Townsend, John J. McAleer, Judson C. Sapp and Arriean Schemer, *Rex Stout: An Annotated Primary and Secondary Bibliography* (New York: Garland Publishing, Inc., 1980).

In the list below, dates given refer to the first completed published version of the novels. Rex Stout published some of his novels, in abridged form, in magazines before they appeared in book form. He published his short stories separately before collecting them in omnibus volumes, and sometimes the titles changed between original publication and their appearance in a collection. The titles given are those adopted when the stories were collected in book form.

I. NERO WOLFE NOVELS

Fer-de-Lance. New York: Farrar and Rinehart, 1934.

The League of Frightened Men. New York: Farrar and Rinehart, 1935.

The Rubber Band. New York: Farrar and Rinehart, 1936.

The Red Box. New York: Farrar and Rinehart, 1937.

Too Many Cooks. New York: Farrar and Rinehart, 1938.

Some Buried Caesar. New York: Farrar and Rinehart, 1939.

Over My Dead Body. New York: Farrar and Rinehart, 1940.

Where There's A Will. New York: Farrar and Rinehart, 1940.

The Silent Speaker. New York: Viking, 1946.

Too Many Women. New York: Viking, 1947.

And Be A Villain. New York: Viking, 1948.

The Second Confession. New York: Viking, 1949.

In the Best Families. New York: Viking, 1950.

Murder By the Book. New York: Viking, 1951.
Prisoner's Base. New York: Viking, 1952.
The Golden Spiders. New York: Viking, 1953.
The Black Mountain. New York: Viking, 1954.
Before Midnight. New York: Viking, 1955.
Might As Well Be Dead. New York: Viking, 1956.
If Death Ever Slept. New York: Viking, 1957.
Champagne for One. New York: Viking, 1958.
Plot It Yourself. New York: Viking, 1959.
Too Many Clients. New York: Viking, 1960.
The Final Deduction. New York: Viking, 1961.
Gambit. New York: Viking, 1962.
The Mother Hunt. New York: Viking, 1964.
A Right to Die. New York: Viking, 1964.
The Doorbell Rang. New York: Viking, 1965.
Death of a Doxy. New York: Viking, 1966.
The Father Hunt. New York: Viking, 1968.
Death of a Dude. New York: Viking, 1969.
Please Pass the Guilt. New York: Viking, 1973.
A Family Affair. New York: Viking, 1975.

II. NERO WOLFE NOVELLA COLLECTIONS AND SHORT STORY COLLECTIONS

Black Orchids. New York: Farrar and Rinehart, 1942. Includes "Black Orchids" and "Cordially Invited to Meet Death."

Not Quite Dead Enough. New York: Farrar and Rinehart, 1944. Includes "Not Quite Dead Enough" and "Booby Trap."

Trouble in Triplicate. New York: Viking, 1949. Includes "Help Wanted, Male," "Before I Die," and "Instead of Evidence."

Three Doors to Death. New York: Viking, 1950. Includes "Man Alive," "Omit Flowers" and "Door to Death."

Curtains for Three. New York: Viking, 1951. Includes "The Gun with Wings," "Bullet for One," and "Disguise for Murder."

Triple Jeopardy. New York: Viking, 1952. Includes "Home to Roost," "The Cop Killer," and "The Squirt and the Monkey."

Three Men Out. New York: Viking, 1954. Includes "Invitation to Murder," "The Zero Clue," and "This Won't Kill You."

Three Witnesses. New York: Viking, 1956. Includes "The Next Witness," "When a Man Murders," and "Die Like a Dog."

Three for the Chair. New York: Viking, 1957. Includes "A Window for Death," "Immune to Murder," and "Too Many Detectives."

And Four to Go. New York: Viking, 1958. Includes "Christmas Party," "Easter Parade," "Fourth of July Picnic," and "Murder is No Joke."

Three at Wolfe's Door. New York: Viking, 1960. Includes "Poison à la Carte," "Method Three for Murder," and "The Rodeo Murder."

Homicide Trinity. New York: Viking, 1962. Includes "Eeny Meeny Murder Mo," "Death of a Demon," and "Counterfeit for Murder."

Trio for Blunt Instruments. New York: Viking, 1964. Includes "Kill Now—Pay Later," "Murder is Corny," and "Blood Will Tell."

III. OTHER DETECTIVE NOVELS BY REX STOUT

The Hand in the Glove. New York: Farrar and Rinehart, 1937.

Double for Death. New York: Farrar and Rinehart, 1939.

Red Threads in *The Mystery Book* (a collection of crime novels). New York: Farrar and Rinehart, 1939, pp. 343–598.

Bad for Business in *The Second Mystery Book* (also a collection). New York: Farrar and Rinehart, 1940, pp. 267–471.

The Broken Vase. New York: Farrar and Rinehart, 1941.

Alphabet Hicks. New York: Farrar and Rinehart, 1941.

Index